simple stitches: Knitting

simple stitches: Knitting

25 PROJECTS
FOR THE NEW KNITTER

VAL PIERCE

LARK CRAFTS

A Division of Sterling Publishing, Co., Inc.
New York / London

Senior Editor: Corinne Masciocchi
Photography: Mark Winwood
Design concept: Beverly Price, www.one2six.com
Production: Laurence Poos
Editorial Direction: Rosemary Wilkinson
Reproduction by Modern Age Repro House Ltd, Hong Kong
Cover Design: Megan Kirby

Library of Congress Cataloging-in-Publication Data

Pierce, Val.
 Simple stitches : knitting 25 projects for the new knitter / Val Pierce. – 1st ed.
     p. cm.
 Includes index.
 ISBN 978-1-60059-902-6 (pb-pbk. with flaps : alk. paper)
 1. Knitting–Patterns. I. Title.

 TT825.P492 2010
 746.43'2041–dc22

                                        2010019171

10 9 8 7 6 5 4 3 2 1

First Edition

Published by Lark Books, A Division of
Sterling Publishing Co., Inc.
387 Park Avenue South, New York, NY 10016

First Published in the UK 2010 by
New Holland Publishers (UK) Ltd
London • Cape Town • Sydney • Auckland
Text copyright © 2010 Val Pierce
Copyright © 2010 photographs and illustrations:
New Holland Publishers (UK) Ltd
Copyright © 2010 New Holland Publishers (UK) Ltd

Distributed in Canada by Sterling Publishing,
c/o Canadian Manda Group, 165 Dufferin Street
Toronto, Ontario, Canada M6K 3H6

Distributed in the United Kingdom by GMC Distribution Services,
Castle Place, 166 High Street, Lewes, East Sussex, England BN7 1XU

Distributed in Australia by Capricorn Link (Australia) Pty Ltd.,
P.O. Box 704, Windsor, NSW 2756 Australia

If you have questions or comments about this book, please contact:
Lark Books
67 Broadway
Asheville, NC 28801
828-253-0467

Manufactured in Singapore

ISBN 13: 978-1-60059-902-6

For information about custom editions, special sales, premium and corporate
purchases, please contact Sterling Special Sales Department at 800-805-5489
or specialsales@sterlingpub.com.

For information about desk and examination copies available to college and
university professors, requests must be submitted to academic@larkbooks.com.
Our complete policy can be found at www.larkbooks.com.

contents

Introduction

I wrote this book with the intention of giving you an insight into the wonderful world of knitting. In this day and age of mass production you may wonder if it's still worth learning to knit. My answer is a resounding yes! It's a great and often inexpensive craft which will provide you with hours of fun and relaxation, and beautiful one-off pieces for you and your friends and family to enjoy.

Knitters are such a diverse breed, ranging from young children with their first hesitant steps when they begin using knitting needles, through to teenagers knitting iPod covers and funky scarves. Mothers and grandmothers knit lovingly for their babies, and young adults can make bags and all manner of accessories, safe in the knowledge that theirs will be unique and different to anything their friends own.

Once you get the techniques of knitting, you'll find that it is a relaxing hobby that is just as easy to do on your own as it is in a group. In recent years, knitting clubs have sprung up in every corner of the world, attracting people of all ages and backgrounds – even the rich and famous love to knit! It is a craft that is experiencing a much-welcomed and deserved revival.

Of course, you could just go out and purchase a garment, bag, or accessory – and that's fine if functionality is the only intention. But there is nothing quite like planning your next project: the excitement of looking through patterns, the sensual pleasure of touching all the luxurious yarns available, the huge palette of colors and textures… And then there's the thrill of anticipation as you work away and watch the piece grow under your very eyes!

With this in mind, the projects in this book are made using the most delightful yarns in beautiful, feminine colors (though of course you are free to choose whichever shades suit your coloring best). The projects range from simple designs for beginners right through to more adventurous pieces. Each of the 25 designs is star-rated and listed in order of difficulty so that you can quickly and easily choose which one will be right for your level of experience – why not work your way through the book!

I hope you have as much fun experimenting with the variety of designs, stitches, and yarns as I have!

Val Pierce

the basics

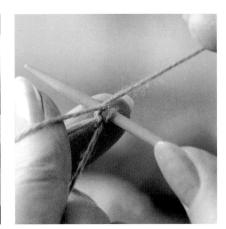

Materials

As with all good recipes, the ingredients go a very long way to the success of the finished product. Substitute the word "ingredients" for "materials" and the same principle applies to knitting. Once you have found a pattern that you want to knit, you need to ensure you have all the necessary equipment and materials to get you started.

Yarns

Yarns come in different thicknesses, weights or ply, and also differ in fiber content. In essence, there are two main types of fiber: man-made and natural. Wool, cotton, silk, angora, alpaca, and cashmere are all natural fibers – beautiful to handle but usually quite expensive. Metallic yarns, nylon and polyester, to mention but a few, are all man-made fibers. These are often blended with naturals to give hard-wearing and practical yarns that are cheaper to buy than natural fibers.

The finest yarns are two- and three-ply (also called baby or fingering); these are usually used for delicate patterns, baby wear, and shawls. Four-ply and double knitting (sport

Knitting needles

Once you have chosen your yarn, you will need some good quality knitting needles to work with. Needles come in three main types: straight single-pointed, circular, and double-pointed, each type having its own special use. Most garments are knitted using straight single-pointed needles; occasionally a circular needle may be needed when picking up large amounts of stitches around front bands on cardigans. Generally though, circular needles are normally used when knitting seamless garments, or where the stitch count needed is too high to fit comfortably on to a straight needle. Double-pointed needles are usually used for making socks and other garments where no seam is required.

or DK) are more widely used for most garments. Next we come on to aran and chunky (medium or bulky) weight yarns, which are very thick and knit up quickly to produce heavyweight, extra warm garments. And last but not least we have the infinite selection of fashion yarns available today. They incorporate ribbons, mixtures of cottons and wools, metallic and many other combinations of fibers and textures that when knitted up produce stunning effects.

Deciding on yarns for a project is quite the task, since these days we are faced with a fantastic array to choose from. A knitting pattern will always state a particular yarn and wherever possible you should follow its guidance, since substituting another yarn will not give exactly the same results. Most yarn store assistants will be able to advise you on yarns should you need help.

There are many needles available in the shops today, ranging from metal, plastic, bamboo, and, at the top end, beautiful and expensive wooden needles. They also come in different lengths as some people like longer needles to work with while others prefer shorter ones; this is all down to personal preference. To begin with, I would suggest buying a set of needles in the middle of the price range; once you are more confident and feel that this is the craft for you, then you can invest in a set of more expensive wooden needles, should you wish to.

Knitting needle size chart

Metric (MM)	US	UK/Canadian
2 mm	0	14
2$^1/_4$ mm	1	13
2$^3/_4$ mm	2	12
3 mm	2/3	11
3$^1/_4$ mm	3	10
3$^3/_4$ mm	5	9
4 mm	6	8
4$^1/_2$ mm	7	7
5 mm	8	6
5$^1/_2$ mm	9	5
6 mm	10	4
6$^1/_2$ mm	10$^1/_2$	3
7 mm	10$^1/_2$	2
7$^1/_2$ mm	11	1
8 mm	11	0
9 mm	13	00
10 mm	15	000

Knitting accessories

There are a number of knitting accessories available, and each one is designed to make a certain task that little bit easier while you are knitting or finishing your garment. I would recommend that you buy some stitch holders, a cable needle, a tape measure, a crochet hook (invaluable for picking up dropped stitches), and a variety of sewing needles, some with large eyes for stitching thick yarn. Yarn bobbins are great when you want to work with small amounts of different colors as they stop the yarns from tangling together. Sharp needlework scissors are very useful to have on hand as is some form of knitting bag or box to keep your work neat and tidy. A row counter will help you remember where you are in your pattern and stitch markers are always a good idea so that you will know where your rows begin and end.

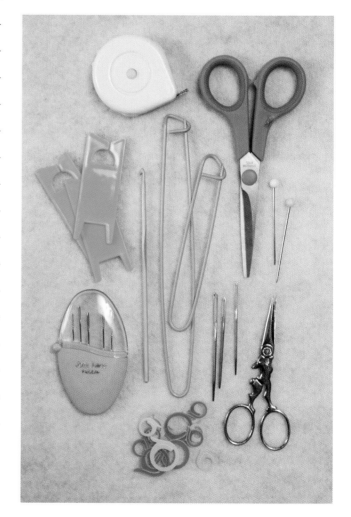

Hints and tips

Knitting takes some practice, and no matter how seasoned a knitter you are, the following hints and tips will help ensure all your projects are a success!

Knitting terminology

When reading a knitting pattern you will notice that the instructions contain a special vocabulary, much of it in abbreviated form. This can be a little puzzling when you first take up knitting, but you will soon get to learn the 'language.' Listed here are the most common knitting terms and their meanings. Some patterns in this book contain abbreviations that are specific to a particular project, and these are listed on the page.

Abbreviations

K = knit

P = purl

K2tog = knit 2 stitches together, thus decreasing a stitch

P2tog = purl 2 stitches together, thus decreasing a stitch

Tbl = through back of loop

Alt = alternate

Beg = beginning

Inc = increase

Dec = decrease

M1 = make a stitch by picking up the strand of yarn that lies between the stitch you are working and the next stitch on the needle and knitting into the back of it, thus increasing 1 stitch.

Rep = repeat

Skp = sl1, k1. Pass slipped stitch over the knitted one.

St = stitch (Sts = stitches)

Sl = slip

Patt = pattern

Psso = pass slipped stitch over

Sl1, k1, psso = slip 1 stitch, knit 1 stitch, pass the slipped stitch over the knitted one

Yfwd = yarn forward, thus making a stitch or a hole in lacy patterns

Yrn = yarn round needle

Yo= yarn over needle

RS = right side of work

WS = wrong side of work

Dpn = double pointed

Ybk = yarn to the back of work

Once you have mastered the basics of knitting you will want to embark on your first project. The time you spend knitting will be better rewarded if you follow just a few general rules. From the experience I have gained over the years, many hints and tips spring to mind; the ones mentioned here are top of my list.

• A major cause of headaches for many knitters is gauge; this small, insignificant word that always appears on patterns, the little square that we all resent wasting precious knitting time making when all we really want to do is get right into a new project! Consistent and exact gauge is what every novice knitter strives to achieve. It is important to get the gauge just right as this is what determines the finished size of the garment and whether it will fit you or end up too large or too small. Taking that extra hour to knit a couple of swatches to get your gauge right is so worthwhile. Mark your sample with pins and keep measuring until you get it right. Make sure you use the correct yarn weight and don't be afraid to change needle sizes from the ones stated.

• Never join a new ball of yarn in the center of a row. Joining at the edge is much neater and will give a more professional finish to your garment. Trying to work in loose ends in the center of a row will give a bulky spot or even a small hole.

• Check back as you work. It is much easier to pull back one or two rows to rectify a mistake than to finish a whole piece, make up the garment and then, horror of horrors, see a huge mistake looking you right in the eye!

• When making a garment, measure the piece you are working on as a rough guide for length, but make sure you always count the number of rows you knit to armholes, on backs, fronts and sleeves before shaping. It is so much easier to match row for row when finishing a garment. Measuring alone can sometimes leave you with as much as four or five rows' difference; you would then either have to ease the seam together or stretch it to fit, or pull it back to correct the row difference.

• Equally important as gauge is "finishing" your garment. Many a beautifully knitted garment has been ruined by poor finishing. Most patterns will tell you the type of seaming recommended for a particular yarn or design. The weight and texture of yarn and stitch pattern can also determine how you should sew up the garment. Matching stripes and lacy patterns, making sure that seams are not puckered, and that ribbing sits flat and aligned are all very important.

Techniques

This section describes the techniques required to teach yourself how to knit. You'll need time and patience to learn and perfect the different techniques, but with practice and determination you'll soon master the basics. It is inevitable that you will make mistakes, but that's all a part of the learning process. You'll find that in no time at all you'll be knitting projects for your family, home, and yourself!

Casting on

The first step in knitting is to learn to cast on. This forms the first row of stitches and one edge of the finished project, usually the bottom edge. There are many ways of casting on. Here are the two most used methods.

Two-needle method

Knitting begins with a foundation row of loops cast on to a needle. The other needle is used to build a series of interjoining loops in rows. Hold the needle with the stitches in your left hand and the needle to make the stitches in your right hand. (Left-handed people should work in reverse.)

1 Make a slip knot about 4 in/10 cm from the end of the yarn and hold the needle in your left hand.

2 Insert the right-hand needle through the front loop and under the left-hand needle.

3 Pass the yarn under and over the point of the right-hand needle.

4 Using the right-hand needle, draw the yarn through the slip knot to form a stitch.

5 Transfer the new stitch onto the left-hand needle, placing it beside the slip knot. Insert the right-hand needle through the front of the new stitch and under the left-hand needle.

6 Take the working yarn under and over the point of the right-hand needle to form the next new stitch. Continue in this way until you have the stated number of stitches.

One-needle or thumb method

This method gives a more elastic edge to the knitting.

1 Unwind sufficient yarn from the main ball to allow you to cast on the stated number of stitches. Wind the yarn twice around the thumb of your left hand.

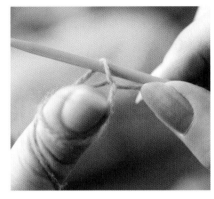

2 Put the right-hand needle through the loop...

3 ... and pull through to form a slip knot.

4 Hold the needle in your right hand, wind the yarn clockwise around your left thumb and hold firmly.

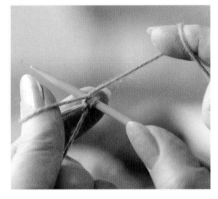

5 Insert the point of the needle through the loop, wind the yarn in your left hand around the back of the point of the needle and in between the needle and your thumb, and pull the point of the needle under the thread, thus forming a stitch.

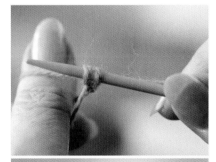

6 Slip the stitch on to the needle close to the slip knot. Your first stitch has been formed. Continue in this way until you have the stated number of stitches.

The knit stitch

Now you have mastered casting on, you can begin to form the first of two fundamental movements in knitting. The knit stitch forms a flat, vertical loop on the knitted fabric face. There are two most widely used methods for forming this stitch, both of which are shown here. Once you can work the knit stitch, you can begin to create a simple lined fabric known as garter stitch (in which you knit every row).

The English/American method

In this method, you use your right hand to pull the yarn around the right-hand needle. The amount of yarn used with each stitch is controlled by winding the working yarn in between your last two fingers. Your left hand moves the knitting forward while your right hand makes the stitch, lifting the yarn, placing it over the needle and pulling it through the loop.

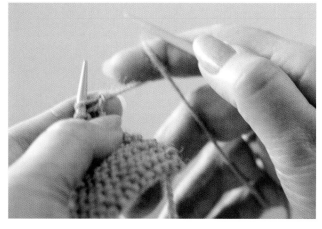

1 Holding the needle with the cast-on stitches in your left hand, wind the yarn around the little finger of your right hand, then under the next two fingers and over the top of your forefinger.

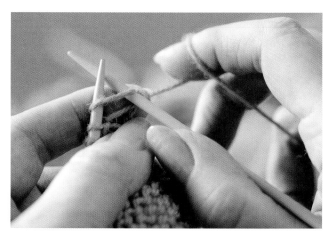

2 Keeping the yarn at the back of the work, hold the second needle in your right hand and insert it into the front of the first stitch.

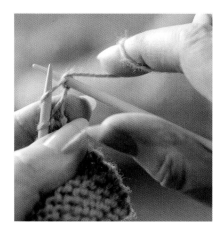

3 With your right forefinger, bring the yarn forward, under and over the point of the right-hand needle.

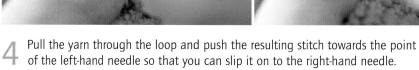

4 Pull the yarn through the loop and push the resulting stitch towards the point of the left-hand needle so that you can slip it on to the right-hand needle.

The Continental method

This method of knitting is often thought to be faster than holding the yarn in your right hand. Instead, you use the forefinger of your left hand to keep the yarn under tension and to pull the yarn on to the right-hand needle. The amount of yarn released, and therefore the tension, is controlled by the fingers. Raising your hand slightly will help to keep the yarn taut.

1 Holding the needle with the cast-on stitches in your right hand, wind the yarn over your left forefinger and lay it across the palm of your hand, then take up the slack between your last two fingers.

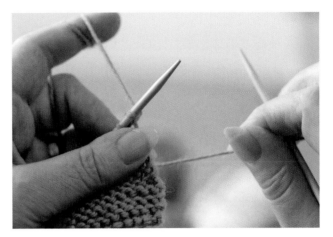

2 With the work in your left hand, extend your left forefinger, pulling the yarn behind the needle. Using your left thumb and middle finger, you will now push the first stitch towards the point and insert the right-hand needle into the front of the stitch.

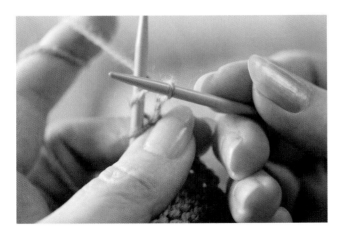

3 Twist the right-hand needle and place the right-hand point under the working yarn to pull the loop on to the right-hand needle.

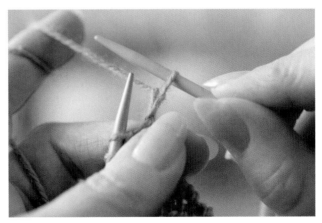

4 It may help to hold the loop with your right forefinger while you pull it down through the stitch. Pull the new stitch on to the right-hand needle.

The purl stitch

The purl stitch is the other fundamental stitch used in knitting. When you use this stitch together with the knit stitch, it will form stocking stitch. This forms a fabric which is flat and smooth on one side and slightly raised on the other. Once you have learned and mastered these two techniques, the stitches will form the basis for a huge range of patterns. The two most widely used methods of forming the purl stitch are the English/American and Continental methods.

The English/American method

With this method the needle is put into the front of the stitch, then the yarn, which is held in the front, is wound over the back of the needle. Purl stitches tend to be a bit looser than knit ones so keeping your fingers close to the work will help to keep the stitches more even.

1 Holding the needle with either the cast-on or knit stitches in your left hand, wind the yarn around your little finger, under the next two fingers and over the forefinger of your right hand.

2 With the yarn in the front of the work, pick up the needle in your right hand and insert the point into the front of the first stitch on the left-hand needle.

3 With your right-hand forefinger, wind the yarn over the point of the right-hand needle and then under it.

4 Pull the loop on the right-hand needle through the stitch and push the new stitch towards the point of the left-hand needle. You are now able to slip the stitch off the right-hand needle.

The Continental method

When using this method, your left forefinger holds the working yarn tight while you pick up the new loop with the right-hand needle. This movement is helped by twisting your left wrist forward to release the yarn and then, using your middle finger, you push the yarn towards the point of the needle.

1 Holding the needle with the stitches in your right hand, take the yarn over your left forefinger, lay it across your palm and take up the slack between your last two fingers.

2 Holding the work in your left hand, push out your left forefinger slightly, pulling the working yarn in front of the needle. Using your left thumb and middle finger, push the first stitch towards the point and insert the right-hand needle into the front of the stitch. Hold the stitch with your right forefinger.

3 Twist your left wrist back slightly, then use the forefinger of your left hand to wind the yarn around the right-hand needle.

4 Push down and back with the right-hand needle to pull the loop through the stitch...

5 ...and slip the new stitch on to the right-hand needle. Straighten out your left forefinger to tighten the new stitch and control the tension.

Casting off

The technique of casting off is used to provide the finishing edge to the end of your work. It is also used when you need to shape pieces of work or to make buttonholes. You would usually cast off on the right side of the work, however patterns will mostly tell you which side to do this.

When following some instructions, you will be told to cast off in the pattern that you are working in, in order to give a particular finish. Don't pull the stitches too tightly when casting off as this could result in a puckered edge or make it difficult when sewing up the garment.

1 Work the first two stitches in pattern. ** With the yarn at the back of the work, insert the point of the needle through the first stitch.

2 Lift the first stitch over the second stitch and then off the needle.

3 Work the next stitch in pattern ** . Now repeat sequence set out between the asterisks until the stated number of stitches are cast off. You will be left with a single stitch at the end of the casting off: slip this off the needle and pull the end of yarn through it quite firmly to secure.

Increasing

When knitting a garment that requires shaping, you will need to add stitches: this technique is called increasing. Using this technique is also necessary when you are creating certain stitch patterns, such as blackberry stitch and lacy patterns. Where increases are made in garment shaping, they are usually worked in pairs so that the piece widens equally on both sides. Where increases are made in decorative patterns, they are combined with decreases so that the stitch count remains the same. There are several methods of making increases in your knitting: the yarn-over method is visible and used in lacy patterns; the other methods are called invisible. In reality, all increases are visible, but some are more obvious than others.

The bar method

This method produces a small horizontal stitch on the right side of the work and is most frequently used. Here, you knit into the front and back of a stitch to make two stitches. This type of increase in widely used on sleeve shaping or on garments where the resulting "bump" will not matter if it shows.

1 Knit a stitch in the usual way but do not take it off the left-hand needle.

2 Insert the point of the right-hand needle into the back of the same stitch...

3 ...and knit again.

4 Take the stitch from the needle in the usual way. The extra stitch formed by this method produces a small bump on the right side of the work and is not very noticeable when worked on the edge of a garment.

Decreasing

When you are knitting you may sometimes have to lose a few stitches in a row, such as when you are shaping an armhole or neckline. Casting off is the usual method used when three or more stitches need to be decreased. If only one or two stitches have to be decreased, you can use any of the methods described here. Decreasings on garments are usually worked in symmetrical pairs (as on a V-neck shaping or raglan sleeve shaping). When the decrease is to the right of the center, the stitch slants to the left;

conversely, if the decrease is to the left of the center, the stitch slants to the right. Right slants are made by knitting or purling two stitches together through the front of both loops; left slants are made by working through the back of both loops. Slip stitch decreases slant in one direction only: from right to left in the knit stitch and from left to right in the purl stitch. Left and right decreases are normally used in the same row.

Right slant (k2tog)

1 Insert the needle in the next two stitches through the front of both loops. Wind the yarn around the needle and pull it through.

2 Transfer the new stitch on to the right-hand needle.

Left slant (k2tog tbl)

1 Insert the needle in the next two stitches through the back of both loops. Wind the yarn around the needle.

2 Pull the thread through and transfer the new stitch on to the right-hand needle.

The slip stitch decrease

This method gives a slightly looser decrease than when knitting two stitches together. If used on a knit row, the decrease slants from right to left and is usually abbreviated as "sl1, k1, psso." On a purl row, a similar decrease can be made, when the decrease slants from left to right. In this case, the abbreviation used is "sl1, p1, psso."

On a knit row

1 Slip one stitch knitwise from the left-hand needle on to the right-hand needle, then knit the next stitch.

2 Insert the left-hand needle into the front of the slipped stich and pull it over the knitted one.

3 The right-to-left slant made by this decrease in a knit row is used on the right side of the center of the work.

Cable knitting

Using cables in your knitting will transform an otherwise plain and simple garment into something quite stunning. Aran patterning demonstrates how cables can be used on a single panel or repeated on the entire project to form an all-over design. The basis of all cable patterns is a simple technique, whereby stitches are crossed over another group of stitches in the same row and some of the stitches making up the cable are either held at the back or the front of the knitting on a special double-pointed cable needle, while the other stitches are knitted. The stitches on the cable needle are then knitted, forming a twist in the knitted fabric. Cables can be worked over many different stitches. Most patterns will state how to work a particular cable in their set of abbreviations.

Right-hand cable

Holding the stitches on a cable needle at the front of the work will always produce a right-over-left cable.

1 Slip the first three stitches onto a cable needle and hold at the front of the work.

2 Knit the next three stitches on the main needle.

Left-hand cable

Holding the stitches on a cable needle at the back of the work will always produce a left-over-right cable.

1 Slip the first three stitches onto the cable needle and hold at the back of the work.

2 Knit the next three stitches on the main needle.

Picking up stitches

When making garments there are always neckbands, collars and possibly edgings that will facilitate the need to pick up stitches from the edge of the knitted fabric. These stitches need to be picked up evenly all around the edge to give a neat, uniform finish to neckbands and collars. Where front bands need to picked up, it is always advisable to measure and divide the stitches equally on the front and back neck so that the bands lie flat when knitted.

To pick up a stitch from an edge

3 To complete, knit the three stitches held on the cable needle.

1 Hold the working yarn behind the completed piece and insert the knitting needle through it, between the rows and between the last two stitches of each row, from front to back.

3 Finally, knit the three stitches held on the cable needle.

2 Wind the yarn over the needle as if you were going to knit a stitch, then pull a loop of the yarn through to form a stitch. Continue in this manner until the stated number of stitches have been formed.

Knitting with more than one color

There are many ways of enhancing your knitting with the use of color. Nowadays, there is a fantastic array of colored and textured yarns available which will make your choice a very exciting one. One of the simplest ways to add color to a garment is to make horizontal stripes, joining in new shades of yarn at the beginnings of rows. Combining different-textured yarns can also produce stunning effects on knitwear, but care must be taken to make sure the yarns are of a similar weight or the gauge produced will vary too much and may spoil your garment. Other ways to incorporate color include block knitting, which entails using separate balls of yarn for each color and then twisting the yarns together at the back of the work when changing colors to avoid making holes. Intarsia is another method and entails the need to use separate balls of yarn for each colored stitch represented on a chart.

Adding new yarn at the start of a row

Use this method when working horizontal stripes.

1 Insert the right-hand needle into the first stitch on the left-hand needle and wind both the old and new yarns over it. Knit the stitch with both yarns.

2 Drop the old yarn and pick up the new yarn, then knit the next two stitches with the short end and the working yarn.

3 Drop the short end of the new yarn and continue knitting in pattern. On the subsequent row, purl the three double stitches in the normal way.

Working from a chart

Colored patterns and designs are often charted on graph paper, making them easy for the knitter to follow. Each square on the chart represents a stitch, and each horizontal line of squares represents a row of stitches. Charts can be either in color or black and white, and have a key at the side with symbols depicting the different shades. Charts are read from bottom to top and usually from right to left. They are usually in stocking stitch, with odd-numbered rows being knit and even-numbered rows being purl. The first stitch of a chart is always at the bottom right-hand corner. Using a straight edge of some kind, like a ruler, under each row will help you keep your place in the chart as you work. There are two methods of carrying yarns across a row when working with more than one color. Both are explained below.

Adding a new yarn within the row

Follow this method when using the original yarn again in the same row. The yarn not in use has to be carried along the back of the work. Use stranding when there are just a few stitches that need to be knitted in a different color (not more than four or five stitches). If the distance between the stitches is more than around five or six stitches, then weaving in is used. Failure to do this will leave long strands of yarn at the back of the work which will spoil the knitted fabric.

1 With the old yarn at the back of the work, insert the point of the right-hand needle into the stitch. Wind the new yarn over the needle and use it as your new stitch.

2 Knit the next two stitches with both the new and old colors.

3 Drop the short end and continue knitting with the new yarn while carrying the old yarn across the back. On subsequent rows, purl the double stitches normally.

Stranding

When using more than one color in a row, the yarn, which is sometimes known as a float, is picked up and carried across the back of the work to make the next new stitch. This yarn should be carried across the back of the work at the same tension as your knitting. If you pull it too tightly, it will pucker the work; if it is left too loose, the work will have holes or larger stitches where the different colors were changed. Much practice is needed to perfect this technique.

Weaving

This method involves the yarn being carried alternately above and below each stitch made so that it is neatly woven into the fabric as you knit. When knitting with many different colors in the same row, winding short lengths of the required yarns on to cards or bobbins will help to avoid tangling as you work. Weaving yarns will give a more dense and less elastic knitted fabric than stranding.

Lacy stitches

Delicate and lacy designs are usually produced by using yarn-over increases. Fine yarns and small needles make lacy patterns ideal for shawls, shrugs or dressy scarves, and are perfect for pretty edgings on garments or bags. Openwork patterns can be used in thicker fabrics too, and these will give a more robust appearance to the garments. The two most widely used methods in openwork patterns are lace and eyelet. Lace is truly openwork, unlike eyelet, which is solid work punctuated by small openings. Lace can be an all-over design or a panel which is then combined with other stitches. Cashmere, alpaca, mohair, silks, and cottons are among the many beautiful yarns that look stunning when knitted in lace patterns.

Openings or holes are formed by the yarn-over increases; these will be offset by the same number of decreases so that the number of stitches remains the same. Eyelets are another form of openwork. When made singly, eyelets can be used as tiny buttonholes or for threading ribbon through and can also be used to form decorative motifs by placing them vertically or horizontally in combination with rows of plain knitting.

Yarn-over in stocking stitch

1 To make a yarn-over in stocking stitch, bring the yarn forward to the front of the work, loop it over the right-hand needle, and then knit the next stitch.

2 The loop and the new stitch are now on the right-hand needle.

3 Knit to the end of the row.

4 On the following row and with the rest of the stitches, purl the loop in the usual way.

Decorative embroidery

Simple embroidery stitches can add color and texture to a knitted garment. There are many stitches to choose from but the one illustrated below is Swiss darning. It is a clever way of transferring a motif onto your knitted garment without having to knit it into the fabric. Much practice is needed to master this technique successfully.

Swiss darning on vertical rows

Bring the needle out on the right side of the work under the strand of yarn at the bottom of a knit stitch. Insert the needle from right to left behind the knit stitch directly above and pull the yarn snug. Insert the yarn under the same strand where the thread emerged for the first half stitch. Bring the needle out under the connecting strand of the knit stitch directly above it.

Swiss darning on horizontal rows

Bring the needle up on the right side of the work under the connecting thread at the bottom of a knit stitch. Insert the needle from right to left behind the knit stitch directly above and pull the yarn firmly. Insert the needle under the same strand where the thread emerged for the first half stitch. Bring the needle up again under the connecting strand of the stitch to the left of it.

Gauge

The importance of tension has already been mentioned so here I will show you how to measure your tension correctly. Obtaining a correct tension is very important to the size and fit of the garment you are knitting so before embarking on a new project, it is imperative you make a sample swatch of at least 4 in/10 cm using the number of stitches and rows stated in the instructions.

Checking your gauge

All patterns quote the gauge needed for the particular item you are knitting at the beginning of the instructions. An example would read:

21 sts x 27 rows over st st = 4"/10 cm.

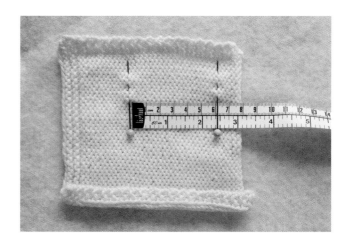

Using this as your guide, make a 5 in/12 cm stocking stitch sample using a few more stitches than stated in the gauge guide (an accurate measurement cannot be taken from edge to edge, so extra stitches will allow you to pin and measure just a few stitches in from each edge). To measure the stitch count, pin the sample right-side down, without stretching it, onto a flat surface, such as an ironing board. You will find it is much easier to count the rows on the reserve side of the work.

Count 21 stitches on your sample and mark with pins, then check this measurement. If there are fewer than 21 stitches to 4 in/10 cm, use a smaller size needle;

if there are more, then use a larger size needle. Each horizontal ridge represents a row of stocking stitch; insert one pin between ridges and count out 27 rows, inserting the second pin in the hollow after the last ridge counted. Using a tape measure, check the measurement of these rows as you did for the width.

Yarn and patterning can also affect gauge, so it's equally important to make a sample if you are changing either one from that of the instructions. When checking gauge on a ribbed pattern, you need to pull the piece out to the correct width before measuring. Don't be afraid to change your needles, as long as the gauge works out correctly, your garment will turn out the right size.

A sample that is too big.

A sample that is too small.

A sample at the correct size.

Correcting mistakes

While you are knitting, it's always a good idea to check your work regularly for any mistakes; the sooner you pick up on them, the easier it will be to correct them. Mark the row where the mistake occurred, then carefully take the work off the needles and pull it back until you are one row above the mistake. Replace stitches back on to the needle by holding the yarn at the back of the work and inserting the left-hand needle into the front row of the first stitch below the unravelled row. To remove the top stitch, pull on the working yarn. Do this very slowly and carefully, since it is all too easy to let the stitch unravel down the fabric. If this should happen, use a crochet hook to retrieve the stitch and work it up row by row, picking up the strand of yarn at the back of the stitch on every row until you reach the top. Carefully slip the stitch back on to the needle and continue working in the normal way.

Finishing and seams

Having created your masterpiece, you will now need to stitch all the pieces together: this is technically termed "finishing." Don't be tempted to rush this step as clumsy seaming can ruin an otherwise beautifully knitted project. Seams should be sewn with a blunt-ended tapestry needle and matching yarns wherever possible. Some fashion yarns containing ribbons and bulky textures are better sewn with a matching finer yarn. Don't use too long a length of yarn at one time, since sometimes the softer yarns can wear thin with continual pulling through the fabric and break.

Match all patterns wherever possible and if you have stripes, make sure they align as you stitch up the seams. Working on the right side of the fabric can make this much easier, since you can see each stripe or pattern in the work as you sew it up. Match ribbing on edging and sleeves, and when stitching on front bands, always pin them in position first, slightly stretching them to give a really neat finish. Garter stitch is better stitched on the right side of the work, matching the little "bumps" as you sew; this will give an almost invisible seam. Backstitching gives a firm seam and a neat ridge inside the garment. Raglan sleeves are simple to stitch in place, however, "set in" sleeves can be a little difficult to sew up. The top of the sleeve is often slightly larger than the armhole, so fold the sleeve in half lengthways and mark the center of the work. Match it to the shoulder seam of the garment and pin it in place. Now pin the pieces together at regular intervals, easing any fullness in the sleeve as you do. Using a fine back stitch seam, carefully sew the sleeve into the armhole.

the projects

baby blanket

An organic cotton is used to make this cute blanket for a baby. A matching cotton lining fabric can be chosen to complement the nursery scheme, making the blanket fully washable. This project is perfect for the beginner, using just knit and purl stitches, but because of the size of the blanket, it will take a little while to complete.

star rating
★★★ (beginner)

measurements
Width: 21½"/55 cm
Length: 27½"/70 cm

materials
- 5 x 1.75 oz/50 g balls of Rowan Perfect Life organic cotton (shade A Khaki)
- 3 x 1.75 oz/50 g balls of Rowan Perfect Life organic cotton (shade B Oyster)
- Pair of 3¾ mm (US 5/UK 9) needles
- Stitch holders
- 20 in/50 cm cotton lining material
- Sewing thread

gauge
24 sts x 30 rows over stocking stitch = 4"/10 cm using 3¾ mm (US 5/UK 9) needles

BABY BLANKET

Using shade A and 3¾ mm (US 5/UK 9) needles, cast on 120 sts.

Work in garter stitch for 5"/12 cm.

Using shade A, knit 26 sts. Slip these sts onto a stitch holder.

Change to shade B and knit to last 26 sts, turn. Slip these 26 sts onto a stitch holder.

Continue on center panel, using shade B and work in st st for a further 18"/46 cm, ending on a purl row. Break yarn and leave these stitches on a holder for the time being.

Now return to the first set of border stitches, join in shade A and continue in garter stitch until strip, when slightly stretched, fits up the side of the blanket, ending with a WS row. Leave stitches on a holder. Repeat with the other border strip.

Next row: Using shade A, knit across 26 sts on the first holder, then across the center panel and finally the other 26 border sts.

Continue in garter stitch on these 120 sts for a further 5"/12 cm.

Cast off in garter stitch.

to finish

Sew the side borders in place.

TO LINE THE BLANKET

Using the knitted piece as a pattern, cut a piece of material the same size, allowing an extra 1¼"/3 cm all around for a hem. Fold in the hem and press all around, then either tack or pin. Now pin the lining onto the blanket and neatly hand stitch it in place all the way round. Press the lining gently when finished.

beaded 'denim' belt

A simple two-row pattern and just two balls of yarn are all that are needed to make this pretty beaded belt. The fringe is very easy to work and adds a little sparkle to the finished piece. Use my color choice or choose a shade of yarn and matching beads to complement your favorite outfit.

star rating
★☆☆ (beginner)

measurements
Width: 2"/5 cm
Length: 52"/132 cm

materials
- 2 x 1.75 oz/50 g balls of Patons Merino Wool DK Denim (shade 00051)
- Pair of 4 mm (US 6/UK 8) needles
- 1 x 5 mm (US 8/UK 6) needle
- 30 x 10 mm crystal beads

gauge
Not critical

BELT

Using 4 mm (US 6/UK 8) needles, cast on 16 sts.
Now commence pattern as follows:
Row 1: K3, p1, *k2, p1* 3 times. K3.
Row 2: K1, *yfwd, k2 (pass the yfwd over the last 2 knitted stitches), k1* 5 times.
These two rows form the pattern and are repeated throughout.
Continue as set until belt measures 52"/132 cm, or the desired length. Cast off.

Beaded fringes

Make 10 pieces, 5 for each end of the belt.
Using 4 mm (US 6/UK 8) needles, cast on 36 sts.
Change to the 5 mm (US 8/UK 6) needle and cast off. The fringe will automatically curl as you cast off.

to finish

Stitch in any ends neatly. Sew 3 beads, evenly spaced onto each fringe, then sew the fringe to the belt ends.

shimmer hairband

Wear this gorgeous hairband to complement your little black dress for that special evening out. Knitted in a metallic yarn using very simple stitches, you can make it in just a weekend. Use my color choices or choose your own from the range available. This yarn unravels very easily so keep a rubber band around the ball while working with it!

star rating
★★★ (beginner)

measurements
20½"/52 cm but will stretch to give a neat fit when wearing it

materials
- 2 x .9 oz/25 g balls of Rowan Shimmer (shade 94 Anthracite) **1**
- 2 x .9 oz/25 g balls of Rowan Shimmer (shade 95 Jet) **1**
- Pair of 4 mm (US 6/UK 8) needles

gauge
24 sts x 34 rows over garter stitch = 4"/10 cm using 4 mm (US 6/UK 8) needles

Note: Yarn is used double throughout

HAIRBAND

Using 4 mm (US 6/UK 8) needles and Jet used double, cast on 20 sts.
Work 20½"/52 cm in garter stitch. Cast off.

Bow

Using 4 mm (US 6/UK 8) needles and Anthracite used double, cast on 20 sts and work 14"/35 cm in stocking stitch. Cast off.

Bow center

Using 4 mm (UK 8/US 6) needles and Anthracite used double, cast on 8 sts and work 4"/10 cm in garter stitch. Cast off.

to finish

Sew the hairband together along the short edge. Sew the bow together along the short edge. Fold the bow so that the seam is in the center. Take the bow center and stitch along the short edge. Thread the bow through the center, and pull out the width to make a nice shape on either side. Secure with a few stitches. Now stitch the bow to the side of band.

evening clutch bag

Add a touch of luxury to a special evening out by making your own pretty clutch bag. Crisp cotton yarn combined with blackberry stitch patterning give a lovely crunchy texture to the finished fabric. The pattern consists of just four rows, making the bag a perfect first project for the novice knitter. I have used autumnal colors for the flower brooch that goes with it but you can choose whichever colors match your outfit or bag.

star rating
★☆☆ (beginner)

measurements
Bag width: 8"/20 cm
Bag depth: 4¼"/11 cm
Brooch: Approximately 2"/5 cm wide

materials
- 1 x 3.5 oz/100 g ball of Patons Cotton DK (shade 712 Black)
- Scraps of DK yarn in four toning shades for flowers
- Scraps of light green and dark green DK yarn for leaves
- Pair of 4 mm (US 6/UK 8) needles
- Pair of 3¾ mm (US 5/UK 9) needles
- 4 large beads
- Brooch pin

gauge
Bag: 22 sts x 30 rows over blackberry stitch = 4"/10 cm using 4 mm (US 6/UK 8)
Brooch: Gauge not critical

special abbreviations
m3 = k1, p1, k1 all into next st

BAG

Using 4 mm (US 6/UK 8) needles, cast on 46 sts.
Now commence pattern as follows:
Row 1: (RS): Purl.
Row 2: K1, *m3, p3tog; rep from * to last st, k1.
Row 3: Purl.
Row 4: K1, *p3tog, m3; rep from * to last st, k1.
These 4 rows form the pattern and are repeated throughout.

Continue until work measures 11"/28 cm, ending on a purl row.
Now work 4 rows garter stitch, and cast off in garter stitch (this is the top edge of the bag and will form the flap).

to finish

With WS of work facing, fold the first 9"/23 cm of fabric in half – the remaining 2"/5 cm will form the flap of the bag. Seam the two short sides neatly. Turn rights sides out. Fold flap over and press very lightly with a cool iron.

BROOCH

Flowers (Make 4)

Using 3¾ mm (US 5/UK 9) needles and appropriate shade yarn, cast on 14 sts.
Now commence pattern as follows:
Work in st st for 4 rows.
Next row: K1, (yfwd, k2tog) to last st, k1.
Next row: Purl.
Work 4 rows in st st.
Do not cast off but run the end of the yarn through the remaining sts, draw up tight and fasten off. Stitch up the side of the flower, then turn right side out, fold the top over to form a cup shape. Secure on base with a few stitches. Sew a large bead in the center of each flower.

Leaves (Make 1 in light green and 1 in dark green)

Using 3¾ mm (US 5/UK 9) needles and green yarn, cast on 3 sts.
Now commence pattern as follows:
**Row 1: K1, inc in next st, k1.
Row 2: Knit.
Row 3: K1, inc in each of next 2 sts, k1.
Row 4: Knit.
Row 5: K1, inc in next st, k2, inc in next st, k1. (8 sts.)
Rows 6 to 10: Knit.
Row 11: K2tog, k4, k2tog.

Row 12: Knit.
Row 13: K2tog, k2, k2tog.
Row 14: K1, k2tog, k1. (3 sts.)**
Work 4 rows garter stitch on these sts.
Now work from ** to **.
Cast off.

to finish

Work in ends on all pieces. Group the flowers together as in the picture, then secure. Place the leaf pieces one on top of the other in a cross, then sew in the center. Stitch the flowers onto the center of the leaves. Finally, stitch the brooch pin onto the back of the brooch.

Using the bag as a template, cut a piece of black lining fabric to size, but allow ⅜"/1 cm all round for the hem. Sew the side seams as with the bag. Insert the lining into the bag and neatly catch it down all around the inner edge of the bag, using a matching thread and a fine hemming stitch.

slouchy hat

In just a couple of evenings you can knit this fun and jaunty little hat, using chunky yarn and large needles. The easy cable band is just 10 stitches in width, and although it's fairly long, it will soon grow.

Star rating

★★★ (beginner)

measurements

To fit an average-size lady's head

materials

- 3 x 1.75 oz/50 g balls of Sirdar Click chunky yarn (shade 157 Baker Boy)
- Pair of 5½ mm (US 9/UK 5) needles
- Pair of 6½ mm (US 10½/UK 3) needles
- Cable needle

gauge

14 sts x 19 rows over stocking stitch = 4"/10 cm using 6½ mm (US 10½/UK 3) needles

special abbreviations

c4b = slip next 2 stitches on to a cable needle and leave at back of work. Knit next 2 stitches in the normal way, then knit the 2 stitches from the cable needle.

c4f = slip next 2 stitches on to a cable needle and leave at front of work. Knit next 2 stitches in the normal way, then knit the 2 stitches from the cable needle.

m1 = make a stitch by picking up the loop that lies between last and next st and working into the back of it.

HAT

Begin with cable band:

Using 5½ mm (US 9/UK 5) needles, cast on 10 sts.

Now commence pattern as follows:

Row 1: K1, p8, k1.

Row 2 (RS): K1, c4b, c4f, k1.

Row 3: K1, p8, k1.

Row 4: K10.

Row 5: As Row 3.

Row 6: As Row 4.

These 6 rows form cable pattern and are repeated throughout.

Cont in pattern until band measures 19¼"/49 cm, ending on a WS row. Cast off.

main part of hat

With RS of work facing and using 6½ mm (US 10½/UK 3) needles, pick up and knit 86 sts evenly along one side of the cable band.

Row 1: Purl.

Row 2 (RS): Knit, increasing 16 sts evenly across row. (102 sts.)

Rows 3–5: Beginning purl work in st st.

Row 6: K6, m1, (k5, m1) to last 6 sts, k6. (121 sts.)

Rows 7–16: Beginning purl work in st st.

Now commence crown shaping as follows:

Row 1: K2, (k2tog, k7) 13 times. K2tog. (107 sts.)

Rows 2–4: Work in st st.

Row 5: K2, (k2tog, k6) 12 times. K2tog, k7.

Rows 6–8: Work in st st.

Row 9: K2, (k2tog, k5) 12 times. K2tog, k6.

Rows 10–12: Work in st st.

Row 13: K2, (k2tog, k4) 12 times. K2tog, k5.

Rows 14–16: Work in st st.

Row 17: K2, (k2tog, k3) 12 times. K2tog, k4.

Row 18: Purl.

Row 19: K2, (k2tog, k2) 12 times. K2tog, k3.

Row 20: Purl.

Row 21: K2, (k2tog, k1) 12 times. K2tog, k2.

Row 22: Purl.

Row 23: K2, (k2tog) across row to last st, k1.

Row 24: P2tog across row. Do not fasten off but run yarn through remaining sts and pull up tight, secure and fasten off. Work in all ends neatly. Sew up with a flat seam. Turn work RS out.

to finish

Do not fasten off but run yarn through remaining sts and pull up tight, secure and fasten off. Work in all ends neatly. Sew up with a flat seam. Turn work right side out.

felted clothespin bag

Keep your clothespins safe in this cute little bag. Knitted in a pure wool chunky yarn and using extra large needles, you will be able to complete it quite quickly. Two delicate little flowers sitting on a leaf decorate this project that's perfect for the novice knitter.

star rating
★★★ (beginner)

measurements (after felting)
Width: 10"/25 cm
Length: 11"/28 cm

materials
- 6 x 1.75 oz/50 g balls of Twilleys Freedom Wool (shade Turquoise) 🧶6
- Scraps of double knitting yarn for flowers and leaf 🧶3
- Small coat hanger
- Pair of 6 mm (US 10/UK 4) needles
- Pair of 4 mm (US 6/UK 8) needles

gauge
10 sts x 14 rows over stocking stitch = 4"/10 cm using 6 mm (US 10/UK 4) needles before felting

Note: The bag can be lightly felted as an option if desired.

BAG

Bag is worked in one piece
Using 6 mm (US 10/UK 4) needles, cast on 40 sts.
Proceed in pattern as follows:
Work 4 rows garter stitch, now change to st st and continue for 18"/45 cm, ending on a purl row.
Divide for opening:
Next row: K10, cast off 20 sts, knit to end.
Turn and proceed on first set of 10 sts.
Next row: Purl.
Work 4 rows in st st.
Next row: Inc 1 st, knit to end.
Next row: Purl.
Repeat last 2 rows 4 times more. (15 sts.)
Leave stitches on a holder.
With WS facing, rejoin yarn to rem sts. Purl to end. Work 4 rows in st st.
Next row: Knit to last st, increase.
Next Row: Purl.
Rep last two rows 4 times more. (15 sts.)
Next row: K15, cast on 10 sts, then k15 on stitch holder. (40 sts.)
Continue on these stitches for a further 7 rows, now work 4 rows garter stitch. Cast off.

Flowers (Make 2)

Using 4 mm (US 6/UK 8) needles and appropriate color, cast on 12 sts.
Commence pattern as follows:
Row 1: Purl.
Row 2: Inc knitways in each stitch to end. (24 sts.)
Repeat last 2 rows once more. (48 sts.)
Cast off loosely.
The knitting will curl as you cast it off. Curl the piece into a flower shape and secure with a few stitches.

Leaf

Using size 4 mm (US 6/UK 8) needles and green yarn, cast on 5 sts.
Commence pattern as follows:
Row 1: Knit.
Row 2: K2, inc (by picking up the strand of yarn between the sts and knitting into the back of it). K1, inc, k2. (7 sts.)
** All increased stitches will be worked as in brackets for this leaf.**
Row 3: Knit.

Row 4: K3, inc, k1, inc, k3. (9 sts.)
Row 5: Knit.
Row 6: K4, inc, k1, inc, k4. (11 sts.)
Row 7: Knit.
Row 8: K5, inc, k1, inc, k5. (13 sts.)
Rows 9 to 11: Knit.
Row 12: K2tog, knit to last 2 sts, k2tog. (11 sts.)
Row 13: Knit.
Row 14: K2tog, knit to last 2 sts, k2tog. (9 sts.)
Row 15: Knit.
Rows 16: K2tog, knit to last 2 sts, k2tog. (7 sts.)
Row 17: Knit.
Row 18: K2tog, knit to last 2 sts, k2tog. (5 sts.)
Row 19: K2tog, k1, k2tog. (3 sts.)
Row 20: K3tog and fasten off.

to finish

Work in all ends neatly. Fold the piece of knitting in half, seam the sides and top, leaving a small opening half way across the top to insert the hanger loop through.

To felt the bag, fill a bowl with very hot water, and add a drop of detergent to open up the fibers and make them more receptive to felting. Wear rubber gloves to protect your hands, then drop the bag into the hot water, swish it around, and squeeze and pummel it to begin the breakdown of the fibers. The fibers will begin to go fuzzy and start to come together. As the bag is only lightly felted, it should take around 30 minutes of pummelling. When the piece is ready, squeeze out most of the water, then wrap the bag in an old towel to remove as much moisture as you can. Now pull the bag quite hard into the shape you require. Cut a stiff piece of cardboard the same dimensions as the bag and slip it inside to give definition to the corners. When you are happy with the shape, lay the bag on a towel in a warm place to dry, overnight preferably.

Once dry, insert the coat hanger and stitch the flowers and leaves on to the side as an embellishment.

toasty slippers

An ideal project for the beginner, these soft and cozy slippers are knitted in simple garter stitch using big needles. You can make them in just a weekend! The flower embellishments are a little more time consuming to make but they are worth the extra effort when they are completed.

star rating
★ ★ ★ (beginner)

measurements
One size (to fit an average lady's foot)

materials
- 3 x 1.75 oz/50 g balls of Twilleys Freedom Wool (shade 420 Olive)
- Scraps of contrasting yarn in DK weight for flowers
- Pair of 6 mm (US 10/UK 4) needles
- Pair of 4 mm (US 6/UK 8) needles
- 2 decorative buttons

gauge
14 sts x 20 rows over stocking stitch = 4"/10 cm using 6 mm (US 10/UK 4) needles

LEFT SLIPPER

With 6 mm (US 10/UK 4) needles, cast on 48 sts, knit 1 row.
Next row: (K2, m1, k1) twice, knit to last 6 sts, (k1, m1, k2) twice. (52 sts.)
Next row: Knit.
Repeat the last 2 rows once more. (56 sts.)
Next row: K25, (k1, m1) 6 times, knit to end. (62 sts.)
Knit 12 rows.

Shape foot

Next row: K19, (k2tog) 12 times, knit to end. (50 sts.)
Next row: K33, turn.
Next row: (K2tog) 8 times, k1, turn.
Next row: K10, turn.
Next row: (K2tog) 5 times, knit to end.
Knit 1 row, cast off fairly loosely knit-wise.

Strap

Count 9 sts in from back seam, pick up and knit 4 sts from cast-off edge.
Working on these 4 sts, continue in garter stitch for 22 rows.
Next row: K2, yrn twice, k2.
Next row: K2, drop extra loop of yrn, knit it and the next st together, k1.
Next row: (K2tog) twice.
Next row: K2tog and fasten off.

RIGHT SLIPPER

Work as left slipper but remember to pick up and knit the stitches for the strap on the opposite side of the foot.

FLOWER (Make 2)

Using 4 mm (US 6/UK 8) needles and DK weight yarn, cast on 57 sts.
Row 1: Purl.
Row 2: K2, *k1, slip this st back onto left-hand needle, lift the next 8 sts on left-hand needle over this st and off the needle, yo twice, knit the first st again, k2. Rep from *.
Row 3: K1, *p2tog, (k1, k1tbl) into loops made on previous row, p1. Repeat from * to last st, k1.
Do not cast off, run yarn through stitches on needle and draw up into a circle to form flower. Sew edge together.

to finish

Work in all ends neatly. Sew the foot seam of the slipper. Attach a button to correspond with the buttonhole in the strap. Stitch a flower to the center front of each slipper.

cuddle cowl

Cuddle up into this soft and snugly cowl on cold winter days. Knitted in a deliciously soft yarn and using bright colored stripes, it will be sure to cheer up even the most dull day. Large needles and an easy 2-row pattern make it quick and easy to complete, even for the novice knitter.

star rating
★★☆ (intermediate)

measurements
Width: 20"/50 cm
Length: 22"/55 cm

materials
- 5 x 1.75 oz/50 g balls of Patons Pompero Aran weight yarn (shade 00070 Lime)
- 4 x 1.75 oz/50 g balls of Patons Pompero Aran weight yarn (shade 00032 Ruby) 4
- Pair of 5 mm (US 8/UK 6) needles

gauge
13 sts = 4"/10 cm in width using 5 mm (US 8/UK 6) needles

Note: When working the pattern, be careful not to drop stitches since the lacy patterning makes it very difficult to pick them up.

COWL

Using 5 mm (US 8/UK 6) needles and Lime, cast on 73 sts. Work 4 rows in garter stitch. Now commence pattern as follows:

Row 1 (RS): K1, (yfwd, sl 1, k2togtbl, psso, yfwd, k next st 1 row below st on needle, letting st above drop off needle in the usual way) to last 4 sts, yfwd, sl 1, k2togtbl, psso, yfwd, k1.

Row 2: K1, Purl to last st, k1.

These 2 rows form the pattern and are repeated throughout.

Work 2"/5 cm in Lime, join in Ruby, work 2"/5 cm in Ruby.

Continue working in stripes of Lime and Ruby as above until you have 6 Lime stripes and 5 Ruby stripes. Do not break off and join in yarn but take it up the side of the work catching it in as you work. Work should now measure approx 22"/55 cm and you will end on a Row 2 of a Lime stripe. Work 4 rows garter stitch in Lime, then cast off.

to finish

Work in all ends neatly. Sew seam of cowl, matching stripes carefully as you do so.

hearts and roses doorstop

Create this pretty doorstop for your home in just a couple of evenings. I have used pastel shades but you can choose colors to tie in with your own decor. A very simple project, using thick yarn and large needles, this doorstop is perfect for the advanced beginner. Embellish it with hearts and roses, knitted in toning shades.

star rating
★★ (intermediate)

measurements
Height: 7"/18 cm
Width: 6"/15 cm
Depth: 5"/13 cm

materials
- 1 x 3.5 oz/100 g ball of Stylecraft Supersoft Baby Aran (Pale blue)
- 1 x 3.5 oz/100 g ball of Stylecraft Supersoft Baby Aran (Cream) 4
- Pair of 5 mm (US 8/UK 6) needles
- Pair of 4 mm (US 8/UK 6) needles
- Scraps of medium yarn in pale green and dusky pink 4
- Scraps of DK yarn in pinks and dark green for roses and leaves 3
- Padded and weighted liner

gauge
18 sts x 25 rows over moss stitch = 4"/10 cm using 5 mm (US 8/UK 6) needles

DOORSTOP
Main strip
Using Pale blue and 5 mm (US 8/UK 6) needles, cast on 27 sts.
Now commence pattern as follows:
Row 1: *K1, p1. Rep from * to last st, k1.
Row 1 is repeated for moss stitch pattern. Cont in moss stitch for 25"/63 cm. Cast off.

Side panels (Make 2)
Using Cream and 5 mm (UK 6/US 8) needles, cast on 23 sts. Cont in moss stitch as for main strip until work measures 7"/18 cm. Cast off.

Handle
Using pale green yarn and 5 mm (US 8/UK 6) needles, cast on 60 sts. Work in garter stitch for 8 rows. Cast off.

Large heart (Make 1)
Using dusky pink yarn and 5 mm (US 8/UK 6) needles, cast on 3 sts.
Row 1: Inc, k1, inc.
Row 2: Purl.
Row 3: Inc, k3, inc.
Row 4: Purl.
Row 5: Inc, k5, inc.
Continue increasing as before until you have 19 sts, ending in purl.
Work 4 rows st st.
Next row: K2tog, k7, turn.
**Next row: P2tog, purl to last 2 sts, p2tog.
Next row: K2tog, k2, k2tog.
Cast off rem 4 sts.
Rejoin yarn to sts, k2tog, knit to last 2 sts, k2tog.
Now complete as first side from **.

Small heart (Make 1 in Pale blue and 1 in pale green)
As large heart until 15 sts, ending in purl.
Work 2 rows st st.
Next row: K2tog, k5, turn.
Next row: P2tog, p2, p2tog.
Cast off.
Rejoin yarn to sts, k2tog, k4, k2tog.
Next row: P2tog, p2, p2tog.
Cast off.

Rose (Make 3 in different colors)
Using appropriate color and 4 mm (US 6/UK 8) needles, cast on 12 sts.
Next row: Purl.
Next row: Inc in each st to end. (24 sts.)
Next row: Purl.
Next row: Inc in each st to end. (48 sts.)
Next row: Purl.
Cast off.

Leaf (Make 2)
Using dark green yarn and 4 mm (US 6/UK 8) needles, cast on 5 sts.
Knit 2 rows.
Inc in first and last st on next and following alt row. (9 sts.)
Now work 7 rows straight.
Dec 1 st each end every row until 3 sts remain.
Next row: K3tog. Fasten off.

to finish

Work in all ends. Seam the main strip along the short ends. Slip onto padded liner. Stitch the handle in place under the top part of the strip (use picture as guide). Now pin one side panel in place and sew seams. Pin and sew other side panel in place; you will now have encased the padded liner. Take the large heart and stitch in place on the front panel. Sew a small heart to each side panel in the centers. Pin roses and leaves in place on large heart, stitch in position.

flap-over gloves

Using a random-dyed yarn, create an instant Fair Isle effect on these pretty fingerless, flap-over gloves. When you need your fingers free, just flip back the mitten tops. A decorative rib adds extra interest to the project. The gloves are not difficult to make, but a little time and patience is needed when knitting the fingers.

star rating
★ ★ ★ (intermediate)

measurements
One size (to fit an average lady's hand)

materials
- 2 x 1.75 oz/50 g balls of Sirdar Crofter DK (shade 0059 Rambler Rose)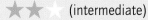
- Pair of 3¾ mm (US 5/UK 9) needles
- Pair of 4 mm (US 6/UK 8) needles
- 2 matching buttons

gauge
22 sts x 28 rows over stocking stitch = 4"/10 cm using 4 mm (US 6/UK 8) needles

RIGHT HAND

Using 3¾ mm (US 5/UK 9) needles, cast on 42 sts.

Work in k2, p2 twisted rib as follows:

Row 1: K2tbl, *p2, k2tbl. Rep from * to end.

Row 2: P2tbl, *k2, p2togtbl. Rep from * to end.

Rep these 2 rows for 4"/10 cm, ending with a Row 1.

Next row: Purl, but increase 4 sts evenly across the row. (46 sts.)

Change to 4 mm (US 6/UK 8) needles and st st, begin knit, work 4 rows in st st. ****

Now shape thumb gusset as follows:

Row 1: K23, m1, k3, m1, knit to end.

Work 3 rows straight in st st.

Row 5: K23, m1, k5, m1, knit to end.

Row 6 and every following alt row: Purl.

Row 7: K23, m1, k7, m1, knit to end.

Continue to inc 2 sts as set in every following alt row to 58 sts.

Next row: Purl.

Divide work for thumb.

Next row: K38, turn.

Next row: P15, turn.

Work on these stitches only for a further 14 rows.

Next row: K1, (k2tog) 7 times, do not fasten off, run yarn through sts left and draw up tightly, then fasten off.

With RS facing, rejoin yarn at base of thumb and knit to end. (43 sts.)

Work 11 rows without shaping ending purl.

** Divide work for fingers.

First finger

Next row: K28, turn and cast on 2 sts.

Next row: Purl 13 sts.

Working on these 15 sts, work 2 rows st st.

Now work 2 rows garter stitch and cast off loosely as before.

Second finger

With RS facing, rejoin yarn, pick up and knit 2 sts from cast on sts at base of first finger, k5, turn.

Next row: Purl 12 sts, turn and cast on 2 sts.

Working on these 14 sts, work 2 rows st st.

Now work 2 rows garter stitch and cast off loosely as before.

Third finger

With RS facing, rejoin yarn, pick up and knit 2 sts from cast on sts at base of second finger, k5, turn.

Next row: Purl 12 sts, turn and cast on 2 sts.

Working on these 14 sts, work 2 rows st st.

Now work 2 rows garter stitch and cast off loosely as before.

Fourth finger

With RS facing, rejoin yarn, pick up and knit 2 sts from cast on sts at base of third finger, k4, turn.

Next row: Purl to end. (12 sts.) Working on these sts only, work 2 rows st st.

Now work 2 rows garter stitch and cast off loosely as before.

LEFT HAND

Using 3¾ mm (US 5/UK 9) needles, cast on 42 sts. Work as right hand glove to ****.

Now shape thumb gusset as follows:

Row 1: K20, m1, k3, m1, knit to end.

Work 3 rows without shaping.

Row 5: K20, m1, k5, m1, knit to end.

Row 6 and every following alt row: Purl.

Row 7: K20, m1, k7, m1, knit to end.

Continue to inc 2 sts as set in every following alternate row to 58 sts.

Next row: Purl.

Divide work for thumb.

Next row: K35, turn.

Next row: P15, turn.

Work on these stitches only for a further 14 rows.

Next row: K1, (k2tog) 7 times, do not fasten off, run yarn through sts left and draw up tightly, then fasten off.

With RS facing, rejoin yarn at base of thumb and knit to end. (43 sts.)

Work 11 rows without shaping.

Now complete as for right hand glove from **.

MITTEN TOPS (Make 2)

Using 4 mm (US 6/UK 8) needles, cast on 44 sts.
Now commence pattern as follows:
Work 6 rows in garter stitch, but decrease 1 st in center of 6th row. (43 sts.)
Now continue in st st for a further 14 rows.
Shape top as follows:

Next row: K1, (sl, k1, psso, k16, k2tog, k1) twice.

Next row and every following alternate row: Purl.

Next row: K1, (sl, k1, psso, k14, k2tog, k1) twice.
Continue in this way, decreasing 4 sts on every alternate row until you have 27 sts left on the needle, end on a purl row.
Cast off.

to finish

Turn right sides inside, stitch up seams of fingers, working in ends of yarn as you go. Join the main seam of the gloves neatly. Turn right sides out. Stitch the side seam of the mitten tops, turn the right sides out and sew half of the mitten to the back of the glove 6 rows below the start of finger shaping. If you like, you can make a small button loop, depending on the size of the button you choose. Attach the button loop to the center of the glove. Sew the button to the back of the glove to correspond with the loop when the mitten top is folded back.

polo neck sweater

Keep nice and cozy in this figure-hugging ribbed sweater with a deep turnover collar and three-quarter length sleeves. It will look equally good over a skirt or jeans! Worked in a wide rib pattern that is very simple to follow, even the less experienced knitter will be able to complete this project.

star rating
★★★ (intermediate)

measurements
Bust size: 34–36"/86–92 cm
Length from back neck to hem: 25"/64 cm
Sleeve length: 13"/33 cm

materials
- 10 x 1.75 oz/50 g balls of Patons Merino wool DK (shade 00032)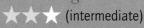
- Pair of 3¾ mm (US 5/UK 9) needles
- Pair of 4 mm (US 6/UK 8) needles
- Stitch holders

gauge
22 sts x 30 rows over stocking stitch = 4"/10 cm using 4 mm (US 6/UK 8) needles

tip When measuring the length of the pieces, pull out to the correct width on a flat surface as rib patterns tend to draw the work in.

BACK

Using 3¾ mm (US 5/UK 9) needles, cast on 103 sts. Now commence pattern as follows:

Row 1 (RS): K2, *p3, k3. Rep from * to last 5 sts, p3, k2.

Row 2: P2, *k3, p3. Rep from * to last 5 sts, k3, p2.

Repeat the last 2 rows 7 times more.

Change to 4 mm (US 6/UK 8) needles and continue in rib as set until work measures 18"/45 cm, ending on a WS row (pull out piece to size before measuring the length).

Shape armholes

Cast off 3 sts in pattern at the beginning of the next 2 rows.

Decrease 1 st at each end of next 7 rows, then every alternate row until 75 sts remain. ****

Work straight until armhole measures 7"/18 cm, ending with a WS row.

Shape shoulders

Cast off 5 sts in pattern at the beginning of the next 6 rows, then 3 sts at the beginning of the following 2 rows. Slip the remaining 39 sts onto a holder for the neckband.

FRONT

Work as back until **** is reached.

Work straight until armhole measures 5"/13 cm, ending with a WS row.

Shape neck

Row 1: Work 27 sts and turn, complete this side first.

Decrease 1 st at neck edge of next 5 rows, then every alternate row until 18 sts remain. Work straight until armhole measures the same as back, ending at side edge.

Shape shoulders

Cast off 5 sts at beginning of next and every alternate row until 3 sts remain. Work 1 row and cast off. Slip center 21 sts onto a holder for neckband. Rejoin yarn to neck edge of remaining stitches and work to end. Complete as given for first side, reversing shapings.

SLEEVES

Using 4 mm (US 6/UK 8) needles, cast on 61 sts. Proceed in pattern as set on back for 8 rows. Taking extra stitches into pattern, increase 1 st each end of next and every following 10th row until there are 69 sts on the needle. Proceed without further shaping until sleeve measures 13"/33 cm ending with a WS row.

Shape sleeve top

Cast off 3 sts at the beginning of the next 2 rows. Dec 1 st at each end of the next and following alternate rows until 35 sts remain. Dec 1 st at each end of the next 4 rows. Now cast off 4 sts at the beginning of the next 2 rows (19 sts). Cast off remaining stitches.

Make other sleeve to match.

to finish and make collar

Join left shoulder seam. With RS facing and using 3¾ mm (US 5/UK 9) needles, work across sts on holder at back neck, pick up and knit 24 sts down left neck slope, work across sts on front neck holder, pick up and knit 24 sts up right front neck slope. (108 sts.) Keeping continuity of rib pattern correct, continue until work measures 4"/10 cm. Now change to 4 mm (US 6/UK 8) needles and work until collar measures 8"/20 cm. Cast off loosely in rib pattern. Join right shoulder seam and collar seam. Join side and sleeve seams. Insert sleeves.

kaleidoscope skinny scarf

Worked in a mohair mix DK weight yarn, this pretty scarf is surprisingly quick and easy to knit. The lace pattern has just eight rows and the piece is knitted on large needles, giving a light and airy feel to the finished fabric. As the yarn is random dyed, the colors knit up in very attractive designs, giving the scarf a unique appearance when completed. Just keep knitting until the piece measures the length you require. Hold the work up and it folds neatly into a skinny scarf.

star rating
★★☆ (intermediate)

measurements
Width: 8"/20 cm
Length: 59"/150 cm

materials
- 1 x 5.3 oz/150 g ball of Ornaghi Filati Wonderful (shade 55)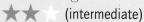
- Pair of 5 mm (US 8/UK 6) needles

gauge
Not critical

SCARF

Using 5 mm (US 8/UK 6) needles and thumb method, cast on 37 sts. Knit 2 rows garter stitch. Now commence pattern with garter stitch edging as follows:

Row 1 (RS): K3, [k1, *yfwd, k3, sl1, k2tog, psso, k3, yfwd, k1*. Rep from * to * 3 times], k3.

Row 2 and all alt rows: K3, Purl to last 3 sts, k3.

Row 3: K3, [k2, *yfwd, k2, sl1, k2tog, psso, k2, yfwd, k3*. Rep from * to * 3 times, ending last rep with k2], k3.

Row 5: K3, [k3, *yfwd, k1, sl1, k2tog, psso, k1, yfwd, k5*. Rep from * to * 3 times, ending last rep with k3], k3.

Row 7: K3, [k4, *yfwd, sl1, k2tog, psso, yfwd, k7*. Rep from * to * 3 times, ending last rep with k4], k3.

Row 8: K3, purl to last 3 sts, k3.

These 8 rows form the pattern and garter stitch edging and are repeated throughout. Continue as set until scarf measures 59"/150 cm, or length required ending on a Row 8. Knit 2 rows garter stitch and cast off. Work in all ends neatly to finish off.

stripy house socks

A blend of merino wool and cashmere gives these comfortable slouchy socks a feel of luxury. They are worked in easy stocking stitch stripes and on two needles instead of the usual four. A decorative rib adds a bit of interest on the turnover cuff.

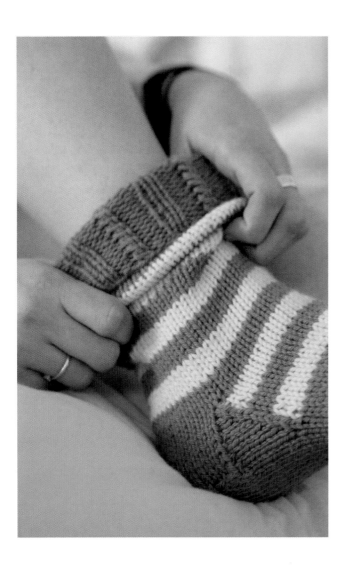

star rating
★★★ (intermediate)

measurements
One size (to fit an average lady's foot)

materials
- 2 x 1.75 oz/50 g balls of RY Cashsoft Baby DK (Sage)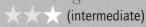
- 1 x 1.75 oz/50 g ball of Cashsoft Baby DK (Limone) 3
- Pair of 4 mm (US 6/UK 8) needles
- Stitch holders

gauge
22 sts x 30 rows over stocking stitch = 4"/10 cm using 4 mm (US 6/UK 8) needles

special abbreviations
tw2b= worked over the next 2 sts as follows, knit into the back of the 2nd stitch but do not slip the stitch off the needle, knit into the front of the first stitch and slip both stitches off the needle at the same time

SOCKS (Make 2 alike)
Using Sage and 4 mm (US 6/UK 8) needles, cast on 52 sts.
Work in fancy rib as follows:
Row 1: *K2, p2. Rep from * to end.
Row 2 (RS): k2, *p2, tw2b, p2, k2.* Rep from * to * to last 2 sts. P2.
Rep the last 2 rows for 2"/5 cm, ending Row 1.
Next row: *K2, p2. Rep from * to end.
Next row: *K2, p2. Rep from * to end.
Continue in k2, p2 rib as on last 2 rows for a further 2"/5 cm, ending with RS facing you for next row. Change to st st and proceed as follows: (carry yarn up side of work when changing colors).
Work in st st stripes of 4 rows Sage, 4 rows Limone until 5th Sage stripe has been completed. Divide for heel. The heel is knitted in Sage so a separate ball of yarn will be needed to enable you to keep continuity of the stripe sequence. Using Sage, knit 13 (for first half of heel), slip next 26 sts onto a stitch holder (for instep). Slip rem 13 sts onto a second stitch holder (for second half of heel).
First half of heel: Return to first set of 13 sts on needle, continue in Sage and proceed as follows:
Row 1 (WS): sl1, p12.
Row 2: K13.
Rep these 2 rows 6 times more, then work Row 1 once more.
Turn heel as follows:
Row 1 (RS): k2, sl1, k1, psso, k1, turn.
Row 2: Sl1, p3.
Row 3: K3, sl1, k1, psso, k1, turn.
Row 4: Sl1, p4.
Row 5: K4, sl1, k1, psso, k1, turn.
Row 6: Sl1, p5.
Row 7: K5, sl1, k1, psso, k1, turn.
Row 8: Sl1, p6.
Row 9: K6, sl1, k1, psso, k1.
Row 10: Sl1, p7.
Break yarn and place remaining 8 sts onto a holder.
Second half of heel: With RS facing, place 13 sts held for second half of heel on needle. Join in Sage.
Row 1 (RS): Sl1, k12.
Row 2: P13.
Rep these 2 rows 7 more times, then work Row 1 once more.
Turn heel as follows:

Row 1 (WS): P2, p2tog, p1, turn.
Row 2: Sl1, k3.
Row 3: P3, p2tog, p1, turn.
Row 4: Sl1, k4.
Row 5: P4, p2tog, p1, turn.
Row 6: Sl1, k5.
Row 7: P5, p2tog, p1, turn.
Row 8: Sl1, k6, turn.
Row 9: P6, p2tog, p1.
Break yarn and place remaining 8 sts on to holder.

Gusset
With RS facing, rejoin Sage and knit 8 sts of first half of heel from holder, pick and knit 6 sts along edge of first half of heel, using Limone, knit 26 sts of instep from holder. Using Sage, pick up and knit 6 sts along edge of second half of heel, knit 8 sts of second half of heel from holder. (54 sts.)
Next row and following alt rows: Purl. **Keep striped color sequence correct on center 26 sts and use Sage either end of row until Gusset is completed.**
Row 3 (RS): k12, k2tog, k26, sl1, k1, psso, k12. (52 sts.)
Row 5: K11, k2tog, k26, sl1, k1, psso, k11. (50 sts.)
Row 7: K10, k2tog, k26, ssk, k10. (48 sts.)
Row 9: K9, k2tog, k26, sl1, k1, psso, k9. (46 sts.)
Row 11: K8, k2tog, k26, sl1, k1, psso, k8. (44 sts.)
Row 12: Purl. Heel shaping is now complete. Continue across all stitches in stripe pattern until you have 10 stripes of Limone in all. Break off Limone and continue in Sage only.

Shape toe
Row 1: K8, k2tog, k2, ssk, k16, k2tog, k2, ssk, k8. (40 sts.)
Row 2 and following alt rows: Purl.
Row 3: K7, k2tog, k2, sl1, k1, psso, k14, k2tog, k2, sl1, k1, psso, k7. (36 sts.) Continue decreasing 4 sts on every other row in this way until 20 sts remain, then cast off.

to finish

Sew in all ends very neatly. Join seams using a very flat seam and matching stripes as you do. Reverse seam for 2"/5 cm at top of sock for turn back.

lacy wrist warmers

The softest cashmere and pure wool are combined with two fairly simple lacy stitches to create these elegant wrist warmers. Wear them to go with your favorite outfit or use them for extra warmth on a cool morning out in town.

star rating
★★☆ (intermediate)

measurements
Length: 8½"/21 cm (to fit an average lady's hand), but the fabric is quite stretchy. If you require a longer finished measurement, just add extra rows before the finishing garter stitch edging, bearing in mind that you may need extra yarn.

materials
- 2 x 1.75 oz/50 g balls of Rowan Cashsoft 4-ply (shade 422 Black)
- Pair of 3¾ mm (US 5/UK 9) needles
- Pair of 4 mm (US 6/UK 8) needles

gauge
Not critical

special abbreviations
skp = sl1, k1. Pass slipped stitch over the knitted one.

WRIST WARMERS
Scalloped edge

Using 3¾ mm (US 5/UK 9) needles, cast on 113 sts.
Now commence pattern as follows:
Row 1: Purl.
Row 2 (RS): K2, *k1, slip this st back onto left-hand needle, lift the next 8 sts on left-hand needle over this st and off the needle, yo twice, knit the first st again, k2. Rep from *.
Row 3: K1, *p2tog, (k1, k1tbl) into yo loops, p1. Rep from * to last st, k1. (42 sts remain.)
Now commence lacy pattern as follows:
Row 1 (RS): K1, *k2tog, yo, k1, yo, skp, repeat from * to last st, k1.
Row 2: Purl.
These two rows form the pattern and are repeated throughout.
When work measures 8½"/21 cm ending on a purl row, change to 3¾ mm (US 5/UK 9) needles and work 4 rows in quite firm garter stitch, then cast off.
Make other wrist warmer to match.

to finish

Note: Side seams will run up the inside of the wrists.
Work in all ends neatly. Sew side seams, remembering to leave an opening for the thumb in the relevant place. Catch together garter stitch rows at top of piece.

trilogy flower brooch

Use up your leftover yarns to create this cute little brooch. Bright colors with matching buttons will cheer up any sweater or jacket, or try metallic yarns and matching buttons to add something different to an evening top. The choices are endless. Although the pattern looks a bit tricky, it's very simple when you try it!

star rating
★ ★ ★ (intermediate)

materials
- Scraps of DK yarn in 4 colors [3]
- Pair of 4 mm (US 6/UK 8) needles
- 2 x 2¾ mm (US 2/UK 12) double-pointed needles
- Brooch pin
- 3 medium buttons
- 3 small buttons

gauge
Not critical

FLOWER (Make 3)

Using 4 mm (US 6/UK 8) needles and DK yarn, cast on 57 sts.

Now commence pattern as follows:

Row 1: Purl.

Row 2: K2, *k1, slip this st back onto left-hand needle, lift the next 8 sts on left-hand needle over this st and off the needle, yo twice, knit the first st again, k2. Rep from *.

Row 3: K1, *p2tog, (k1, k1tbl) into loops made on previous row, p1. Rep from * to last stitch, k1. Do not cast off, run yarn through 22 stitches on needle and draw up into a circle to form flower, sew edge together.

STEM (Make 2)

The stems are made using an I-cord (knitted cord). Although the method sounds a bit complicated when you try it out, you will find it is very simple and quick to do.

Using double-pointed needles and green yarn, cast on 4 sts. Knit the first row. Slide the sts to the opposite end of the needle. The working yarn is
at the bottom of the row. Knit again, pulling the working yarn up the back of the piece so you can knit with it. Again, slide the sts to the opposite end of the needle. Repeat in this manner. As you pull the yarn, the back will close up on itself, like magic. Continue until the piece measures approximately 2"/5 cm, then cast off. Make the second piece the same, but work until piece measures 3"/8 cm, then cast off.

LEAF

Using 4 mm (US 6/UK 8) needles and green yarn, cast on 8 sts.

Now commence pattern as follows:

Knit 2 rows.

Inc 1 st at each end of next and every alt row until there are 16 sts.

Work 8 rows straight in garter stitch.

Dec 1 st at each end of next and every alt row until 2 sts remain.

Next row: K2tog and fasten off.

to assemble

Work in all ends on pieces. Sew the stems to the centers of 2 of the flowers. Now stitch the buttons in the center of each flower – the smaller button on top of the medium button. Sew the two stems to the back of the leaf, then sew the third flower to the front of the leaf. Secure the brooch pin to the back of the leaf.

twilight tea light holders

Bring a touch of romance to your alfresco dining with these delightful tea light holders. They will make a perfect addition to your table setting on a warm summer's evening. Knitted in a shiny metallic yarn, using a simple 6-row lacy pattern, you will be able to complete them in just a weekend. This type of yarn tends to unravel very easily so a handy tip is to keep an elastic band around the ball when you are not using it.

star rating
★★★ (intermediate)

measurements
To fit a mixer glass approximately 9"/22 cm in circumference

materials
- 1 x .9 oz/25 g ball of Madeira Metallic yarn in three shades: silver, gold and bronze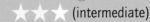
- Pair of 3¾ mm (US 5/UK 9) needles
- Pair of 2¾ mm (US 2/UK 12) needles

gauge
Not critical

Note: Holders need to be a little smaller in circumference than the glass to ensure a snug fit.

Side of holder

This piece is worked sideways.

Using 3¾ mm (US 5/UK 9) needles, cast on 21 sts. Purl 1 row.

Now commence pattern as follows:

Row 1 (RS): K3, yfwd, k2tog, p2, yon, sl1, k1, psso, k3, k2tog, yrn, p2, k1, yfwd, k2tog, k2.

Row 2 and all alt rows: K3, yfwd, k2togtbl, k2, p7, k3, yfwd, k2togtbl, k2.

Row 3: K3, yfwd, k2tog, p2, k1, yfwd, sl 1, k1, psso, k1, k2tog, yfwd, k1, p2, k1, yfwd, k2tog, k2.

Row 5: K3, yfwd, k2tog, p2, k2, yfwd, sl 1, k2tog, psso, yfwd, k2, p2, k1, yfwd, k2tog, k2.

Row 6: As Row 2.

These 6 rows form the pattern for the side of the holder and are repeated throughout. Continue in pattern until work measures 8"/20 cm, ending on a Row 6. Cast off.

Base

Using 2¾ mm (US 2/UK 12) needles, cast on 10 sts.

Knit 2 rows.

Cast on 2 sts at beg of next 6 rows. (22 sts.)

Work 2 rows in garter stitch.

Next row: Inc 1 st each end of next row. (24 sts.)

Cont straight in garter stitch for a further 20 rows.

Next row: Dec 1 st each end of the row.

Work 2 rows more in garter stitch.

Cast off 2 sts at beg of next 6 rows. (10 sts.)

Work 2 rows straight in garter stitch and cast off.

to finish

Work in all ends neatly. Join the short seam on the side piece of the holder, carefully matching the pattern as you do. Take the base and pin in position on the inside of the holder, stitch in place carefully, easing to fit if needed. Slip holder onto glass. Place a tea light inside the tumbler.

For safety reasons, always make sure that lighted candles are never left unattended.

snuggle alpaca shawl

Snuggle into this luxurious shawl, made in the softest baby alpaca yarn. The shawl is made in simple garter stitch, with the addition of a lacy border, which is knitted separately and sewn on. The lace is a simple 8-row pattern repeat but if you can't manage the lace, then leave it out; it will look just as pretty!

star rating
★★☆ (intermediate)

measurements
Width: 56"/142 cm
Depth: 30"/76 cm
Lace edging will add an extra 2"/5 cm on width and depth

materials
- 7 x 1.75 oz/50 g balls of RY Baby Alpaca DK (shade 205 Jacob)
- Pair of 5 mm (US 8/UK 6) needles
- Circular needle size 5 mm (US 8/UK 6)
- Blunt-ended sewing needle

gauge
20 sts over garter stitch = 4"/10 cm using 5 mm (US 8/UK 6) needles

SHAWL

Using 5 mm (US 8/UK 6) needles, cast on 1 st.
Now commence pattern as follows:
Next row: Knit twice into stitch.
Next row: K1, knit twice into next stitch.
Next row: K1, inc in next st, k1.
Next row: K1, inc in next st, knit to end.
Continue to inc 1 st at the beginning of every
row as set until you have 210 sts on the needle.
Cast off. When stitches become too many for
ordinary needles, change to the circular needle
and work back and forth.

Lace edging

Using 5 mm (US 8/UK 6) needles, cast on 12 sts.
Now commence pattern as follows:
Row 1: K3, yfwd, k5, yfwd, k2tog, yfwd, k2.
Row 2: K2, p12.
Row 3: K4, sl1, k2tog, psso, k2, (yfwd, k2tog)
twice, k1.
Row 4: K2, p10.
Row 5: K3, sl1, k1, psso, k2, (yfwd, k2tog) twice,
k1.
Row 6: K2, p9.
Row 7: K2, sl1, k1, psso, k2, (yfwd, k2tog) twice,
k1.
Row 8: K2, p8.
Row 9: K1, sl1, k1, psso, k2, (yfwd, k2tog) twice,
k1.
Row 10: K2, p7.
Row 11: Sl1, k1, psso, k2, yfwd, k1, yfwd, k2tog,
yfwd, k2.
Row 12: K2, p8.
Row 13: (K3, yfwd) twice, k2tog, yfwd, k2.
Row 14: K2, p10.
These 14 rows form the pattern and are repeated
throughout. Continue in pattern until lace strip is
long enough to go around the two side edges of
the shawl, ending on a Row 14. Cast off.

to finish

Work in all ends neatly. Pin edging in place
around the two side edges, gather slightly to
fit around the point of the shawl. Sew in place
using a flat seam.

waves cushion cover

Using a soft merino wool yarn, make yourself a pretty cushion, or even two! The pattern looks much more complicated than it is to knit. When worked, it creates an attractive wavy effect, but is only used for the front of the cushion; the back panels are worked in easy stocking stitch with moss stitch button bands.

star rating

★★☆ (intermediate)

measurements

16"/40 cm square

materials

- 5 x 1.75 oz/50 g balls of Sublime Extra fine Merino wool DK (shade 010 Salty Grey)
- Pair of 4½ mm (US 7/UK 7) needles
- 16"/40 cm cushion pad
- 2 matching buttons

gauge

22 sts x 28 rows over stocking stitch = 4"/10 cm using 4½ mm (US 7/UK 7) needles

FRONT OF CUSHION

Using 4½ mm (UK 7/US 7) needles, cast on 82 sts.
Work 2 rows in st st.
Now commence pattern as follows:
Row 1 (RS): P4, *k9, p4.* Rep from * to * to end.
Row 2: K6, *p5, k8.* Rep from * to * ending p5, k6.
Row 3: P7, *k3, p10.* Rep from * to * ending k3, p7.
Row 4: K8, *p1, k12.* Rep from * to * ending p1, k8.
Row 5: K4, *p9, k4.* Rep from * to * to end.
Row 6: P6, *k5, p8.* Rep from * to * ending k5, p6.
Row 7: K7,*p3, k10.* Rep from * to * ending p3, k7.
Row 8: P8, *k1, p12.* Rep from * to * ending k1, p8.
Row 9: Knit.
Row 10: Purl.
These 10 rows form the pattern for the front and are repeated throughout.
Continue in pattern until work measures approximately 16"/40 cm, ending on a Row 10.
Cast off.

BACK OF CUSHION (Make 2 panels)
Panel 1

Using 4½ mm (US 7/UK 7) needles, cast on 82 sts and work in st st with garter stitch border as follows.
Row 1 (RS): Knit.
Row 2: K2, purl to last 2 sts, k2.
Continue as on last 2 rows until work measures 7½"/19 cm, ending on a Row 2.
Now work 12 rows in moss stitch across all stitches.
Cast off in moss stitch.

Panel 2

Work as Panel 1 until you have completed 6 rows moss stitch.
Next row: (Make buttonholes): work 19 sts, cast off 3, work 38 sts (including st on needle after cast off), cast off 3, work to end.
Next row: Work in moss stitch but cast on 3 sts over the cast-off stitches of the previous row.
Work 4 more rows moss stitch, then cast off.

to finish

Work in all ends neatly. With RS facing, pin Panels 1 and 2 of the cushion back onto the cushion front, overlapping a little for the button band. Sew in place along all the sides using a fine back stitch seam. Turn RS out and attach buttons to correspond with buttonholes.

man's tweed sweater

Knitted in a beautifully soft roving-type yarn with multi-color flecks and unique color shading, this gorgeous chunky sweater is perfect for weekends in the country or relaxing at home. Large needles and thick yarn make it a quick and easy knit. A cross-over V-neck and cable panel on the front add a little extra interest.

star rating
★★☆ (intermediate)

measurements
To fit chest 40-42"/102-107 cm
Actual measurements
Chest: 44"/111 cm
Length to shoulders: 28"/72 cm
Sleeve length: 20"/50 cm

materials
- 9 x 3.5 oz/100 g balls of Patons Shadow Tweed Chunky (shade 6917 Grey/Charcoal mix)
- Pair of 5½ mm (US 9/UK 5) needles
- Pair of 6½ mm (US 10½/UK 3) needles
- Cable needle
- Large-eyed sewing needle

gauge
14 sts x 19 rows over stocking stitch = 4"/10 cm using 6½ mm (US 10½/UK 3) needles

special abbreviations
c12b = worked over 12 sts as follows: slip first 6 sts onto cable needle and leave at back of work, knit next 6 sts, now knit 6 sts from cable needle

Note: The yarn is very soft and will break easily, so when sewing up the garment use multiple short lengths on the seams.

BACK

Using 5½ mm (US 9/UK 5) needles, cast on
78 sts loosely.
Commence rib as follows:
Row 1: (K2, p2) to last 2 sts, k2.
Row 2: (P2, k2) to last 2 sts, k2.
Work 6 more rows rib as set.
Change to 6½ mm (US 10½/UK 3) needles
and proceed in st st until work measures
27½"/70 cm, ending on a purl row.

Shape shoulder

Cast off 13 sts at beg of next 4 rows. Cast off
remaining 26 sts.

FRONT

Using 5½ mm (US 9/UK 5) needles, cast on 78 sts
loosely.
Commence rib as follows:
Row 1: (K2, p2) to last 2 sts, k2.
Row 2: (P2, k2) to last 2 sts, k2.
Work 5 more rows rib as set.
Row 1: (RS) K54, p3, inc in each of next 6 sts,
p3, k12. (84 sts.)
Row 2: P12, k3, p12, k3, p54.
** Row 3: K54, p3, c12b, p3, k12.
Row 4: P12, k3, p12, k3, p54.
Row 5: K54, p3, k12, p3, k12.
Rep Rows 4 and 5, 6 times more. (14 rows in all.)
Next row: As Row 4. **
These 16 rows form cable panel and are repeated
from ** to **.
Cont in pattern as set until work measures
19½"/50 cm, ending on a WS row.
Divide for neck.
Next row: Pattern 36 sts, turn and work on this
side first.
Next row: P2tog, purl to end.
Dec 1 st at end of next and following 4 alt rows.
(30 sts.)
Now dec 1 st at end of every following 4th row
until 26 sts remain.
Cont straight until front matches back to start
of shoulder shaping, ending with RS facing for
next row.

Shape shoulder

Cast off 13 sts at beg of next 4 rows. Cast off remaining 26 sts.

Next row: Purl.

Next row: Cast off 13 sts, knit to end.

With RS facing, join yarn to remaining sts, cast off 6 sts loosely for center neck opening, work to end of row.

Keeping continuity of cable panel, disregarding the extra 6 sts increased in the panel, work neck shaping to match other side, reversing shaping as you do so. **Note:** On final row before shaping shoulder, dec 6 sts across the cable panel.

SLEEVES (Make 2 alike)

Using 5½ mm (US 9/UK 5) needles, cast on 40 sts loosely.

Now commence pattern as follows:

Work 7 rows in k2, p2 rib.

Change to 6½ mm (US 10½/UK 3) needles and proceed with pattern as follows:

Continue in st st, starting with a knit row and at the same time inc 1 st at each end of the 7th row and every following 8th row until you have 60 sts on the needle.

Now inc 1 st at each end of every following 10th row until you have 58 sts.

Continue without shaping until work measures 20"/51 cm or desired length, ending on a purl row.

Shape top

Cast off 3 sts at beg of next 4 rows. Now cast off 4 sts at beg of next 10 rows. (6 sts.)

Cast off.

to finish and make neck border

Join right shoulder seam.

Neck border

With RS facing and using 5 mm (US 8/UK 6) needles, pick up and knit 40 sts down left side of neck. Work in k2, p2 rib until neck border fits along center front cast off sts. Cast off in rib.

With RS facing and using 5 mm (US 8/UK 6) needles, pick up and knit 40 sts from right side neck, and 30 from back neck. (70 sts.)

Work in k2, p2 rib until neck border matches other side. Cast off in rib.

Catch down side edges of border neatly to base of V-neck, right over left. Join neck border and left shoulder seam. Join side and sleeve seams. Insert sleeves.

cashmere evening stole

Wrap yourself in pure luxury with this beautiful cashmere evening stole. Worked in two different Shetland lace stitch patterns, you will need both time and patience to create the project. Always make a note of which row you are working on when taking a break from the knitting so that you can follow on the correct row when you begin again.

star rating
★★★ (experienced)

measurements
Length: 62"/158 cm
Width: 21"/54 cm

materials
- 7 x 1.75 oz/50 g balls of Angel Yarns Cashmere (shade Black)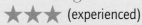
- Pair of 4½ mm (US 7/UK 7) needles

gauge
24 sts x 34 rows over lace pattern = 4"/10 cm using 4½ mm (US 7/UK 7) needles

STOLE

Using size 4½ mm (US 7/UK 7) needles, cast on 120 sts. Knit 8 rows in garter stitch.

Now commence Pattern A as follows:

Pattern A
Row 1 (RS): K4, *k1, k2tog, yfwd, k1, yfwd, k2tog tbl, k1.* Rep from * to * to last 4 sts, k4.
Row 2 and following alt rows: K4, purl to last 4 sts, k4.
Row 3: K4, *k2tog, yfwd, k3, yfwd, k2togtbl.* Rep from * to * to last 4 sts, k4.
Row 5: K4, *k2, yfwd, k3tog, yfwd, k2.* Rep from * to * to last 4 sts, k4.
Row 6: K4, purl to last 4 sts, k4.
These 6 rows form Pattern A and are repeated throughout.

Keep 4 sts each end of every row in garter stitch and work 10"/25 cm in Pattern A, ending on a 6th pattern row.
Now work 4 rows in garter stitch, dec 1 st in the center of the last row. (119 sts.)

Now commence Pattern B as follows:

Pattern B
Row 1 (RS): K5, *yfwd, k3, sl 1, k2tog, psso, k3, yfwd, k1*. Rep from * to * to last 4 sts, k4.
Row 2 and following alt rows: K4, purl to last 4 sts, k4.
Row 3: K5, *k1, yfwd, k2, sl 1, k2tog, psso, k2, yfwd, k2*. Rep from * to * to last 4 sts, k4.
Row 5: K5, *k2, yfwd, k1, sl 1, k2tog, psso, k1, yfwd, k3*. Rep from * to * to last 4 sts, k4.
Row 7: K5,*k3, yfwd, sl 1, k2tog, psso, yfwd, k4*. Rep from * to * to last 4 sts, k4.
Row 8: K4, purl to last 4 sts, k4.
These 8 rows form Pattern B and are repeated throughout.

Continue in Pattern B until work measures 40"/102 cm from beginning of Pattern B, ending on an 8th pattern row.
Work 4 rows in garter stitch, inc 1 st in center of last row. (120 sts.)
Work 10"/25 cm in Pattern A, ending on a 6th pattern row.
Work 8 rows in garter stitch. Cast off. Work in all ends neatly.

day bag

A project for the more experienced knitter, this chunky cabled day bag will take some time and patience to create. Large enough to fit all your everyday needs into, it is sure to become a favorite bag. Made in three separate pieces, the bag is then stitched together and finally edged with a contrasting piping.

star rating
★★★ (experienced)

measurements
Bag width: 14"/36 cm
Bag depth: 8"/20 cm

materials
- 3 x 3.5 oz/100 g balls of King Cole Homespun (shade 482 Slate) **5**
- Scraps of King Cole Homespun (shade 481 Oatmeal) **5**
- Pair of 6 mm (US 10/UK 4) needles
- Pair of 6½ mm (US 10½/UK 3) needles
- Pair of 4½ mm (US 7/UK 7) double-pointed needles
- Cable needles and stitch holders
- 2 large press fasteners

gauge
12 sts x 18 rows over stocking stitch = 4"/10 cm using 6½ mm (US 10½/UK 3) needles

special abbreviations
c6b = slip next 3 sts onto cable needle, leave at back of work, knit next 3 sts, then knit 3 sts from cable needle
c8b = slip next 4 sts onto cable needle, leave at back of work, knit next 4 sts, then knit 4 sts from cable needle
c8f = slip next 4 sts onto cable needle, leave at front of work, knit next 4 sts, then knit 4 sts from cable needle

BAG PANEL

Bag panel is worked sideways (Work 2 pieces alike).

Using 6½ mm (US 10½/UK 3) needles and Slate, cast on 44 sts. Purl 1 row.

Now commence pattern as follows:

Row 1 (RS): P4, c6b, p4, c8b, c8f, p4, c6b, p4.

Row 2: K4, p6, k4, p4, (k1, p1) 4 times, p4, k4, p6, k4.

Row 3: P4, k6, p4, k4, (p1, k1) 4 times, k4, p4, k6, p4.

Row 4: As Row 2.

Row 5: As Row 3.

Row 6: As Row 2.

Row 7: P4, k6, p4, k16, p4, k6, p4.

Row 8: K4, p6, k4, p16, k4, p6, k4.

Row 9: As Row 7.

Row 10: As Row 8.

These 10 rows form the pattern and are repeated throughout.

Cont in pattern for a further 5 repeats.

Next row: As pattern Row 1.

Next row: As pattern Row 2.

Cast off firmly in pattern.

With RS facing, pick up and knit 38 sts evenly across one long edge of a main panel.

Work in garter stitch for 10 rows.

Now divide work for the handle.

Next row: K13, cast off 12, knit to end.

Work on each set of 13 sts separately.

Next 2 rows: Work in garter stitch. Do not break yarn, sl sts onto spare needle. Join in new yarn to remaining 13 sts, knit 2 rows in garter stitch, break yarn. Return to first set of 13 sts, knit across these sts, cast on 12, knit across other set of 13 sts. (38 sts.)

Cont in garter stitch, work 4 rows.

Next 6 rows: Cast off 2 sts, knit to end. (26 sts.)

Work 4 rows garter stitch on these sts, then cast off.

Work other bag panel to match.

Gusset

Using 6 mm (US 10/UK4) needles and Slate, cast on 16 sts and work in garter stitch until piece is long enough to fit all around bag, starting and finishing at point where sts were cast off for shaping the top of the holdall. Remember to slip the first stitch on every row to give a neat edging. Cast off.

Piping for edging handle and opening

The piping is made using an I-cord (knitted cord). Although the method sounds a bit complicated when you first try it out, you will find it is simple and quick to do.

Using 4½ mm (US 7/UK 7) double-pointed needles and Oatmeal, cast on 4 sts. Knit the first row. Slide the stitches to the opposite end of the needle. The working yarn is at the bottom of the row. Knit again, pulling the working yarn up the back of the piece so you can knit with it. Again, slide the stitches to the opposite end of the needle. Repeat in this manner and as you pull the yarn, the back will close up on itself, like magic. Continue until the piece is long enough to fit all around the top of the handles. Cast off. Now make two short pieces: these are to edge the openings for the hand holds in each side of the bag.

to finish

Work in all ends neatly on all pieces. Pin the gusset in place between the two side panels, starting and ending where the shaping for the handle begins on each side. Sew neatly in place. Stitch the piping around the top of the bag and also around each handle opening. Fold the sides of the bag inwards and stitch a press fastener to each one to keep them in place.

hugs 'n' kisses hat

Time and patience will be well rewarded when you complete this pretty hat. Made in a gorgeous pure wool tweed yarn, the stitches used, although fairly simple, give a stunning effect when knitted up. The cable used here is often referred to as 'hugs 'n' kisses' because of the circle and cross formation of the stitches. I suggest taking care when setting the pattern stitches on the first few rows as this will make it easier to follow as you proceed.

Star rating
★★★ (experienced)

measurements
One size (to fit an average-size lady's head)

materials
- 1 x 3.5 oz/100 g ball of Cygnet Truly Wool Rich Aran (shade 0148 Blue Tweed) [4]
- Pair of 3¾ mm (US 5/UK 9) needles
- Pair of 4½ mm (US 7/UK 7) needles
- Cable needle

gauge
18 sts x 22 rows over stocking stitch = 4"/10 cm using 4½ mm (US 7/UK 7) needles

special abbreviations
tw2f = twist 2 front worked over the next 2 stitches. Knit into the front of the second stitch but do not slip the stitch off the needle. Now knit into the first stitch in the normal way and slip both stitches off the needle together.

tw2b = twist 2 back worked over the next 2 stitches. Knit into the back of the second stitch but do not slip the stitch off the needle. Now knit into the front of the first stitch in the normal way and slip both stitches off the needle together.

c4f = slip next 2 stitches on to a cable needle and leave at front of work. Knit next 2 stitches, then knit the 2 stitches from the cable needle.

c4b = slip next 2 stitches on to a cable needle and leave at back of work. Knit next 2 stitches, then knit the 2 stitches from the cable needle.

HAT

Using 3¾ mm (US 5/UK 9) needles and thumb method, cast on 108 sts. Work 8 rows in k2, p2 rib.

Increase row: P9, [inc in each of next 2 sts, p13] 6 times, inc in each of next 2 sts, p7. (122 sts.)

Change to size 4½ mm (US 7/UK 7) needles and commence pattern as follows:

Row 1 (RS): P2, [*tw2f, p1, k8, p1, tw2b*, p3] 7 times, p1.

Row 2: K1, [k1, knit into the front and back of the next st 5 times, then slip 1st 4 of these sts over the end st, thus making a small bobble, k1, *p2, k1, p8, k1, p2*] 7 times, k2.

Row 3: P2, [*tw2f, p1, c4f, c4b, p1, tw2b*, p3] 7 times, p1.

Row 4: K1, [k3, *p2, k1, p8, k1, p2*] 7 times, k2.

Rows 5–10: Rep last 4 rows once, then rep Rows 1 and 2 again.

Row 11: P2, [*tw2f, p1, c4b, c4f, p1, tw2b*, p3] 7 times, p1.

Row 12: As Row 4.

Rows 13–14: As Rows 1 and 2.

Row 15: As Row 11.

Row 16: As Row 4.

These 16 rows form the pattern. Repeat them until work measures 6½"/16.5 cm, ending with a 4th pattern row.

Now commence crown shaping as follows:

Row 1: P2, *patt 3, k2, (k2tog) twice, k2, patt 6; rep from * 6 times, p1. (108 sts.)

Row 2 and all alt rows: P1, (k1, p1) to last st, k1.

Row 3: (Rib 9, p3tog) 9 times. (90 sts.)

Row 5: (Rib 7, p3tog) 9 times. (72 sts.)

Row 7: (Rib 5, p3tog) 9 times. (54 sts.)

Row 9: (Rib 3, p3tog) 9 times. (36 sts.)

Row 11: (K1, p3tog) 9 times. (18 sts.)

Rib 1 row. Break yarn and run end through remaining sts on needle. Draw up and secure.

to finish

Work all ends in neatly. Sew back seam of hat matching rib and patterns.

cottage rose pajama case

A silk and cashmere blend yarn is used to create this pretty, feminine pajama case. The main piece of the project is knitted in double moss stitch, with the addition of an intarsia rose worked into the flap. A delicate lacy edging is knitted separately and sewn on afterwards. The sides are tied with satin ribbon bows.

star rating
★★★ (experienced)

measurements
12"/30 cm square with flap folded over

materials
- 4 x 1.75 oz/50 g balls of Sirdir Balmoral DK yarn (cream)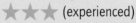
- Scraps in pale pink, rose pink and green for intarsia
- 39"/1 m double-sided satin ribbon in cream
- Pair of 4 mm (US 6/UK 8) needles
- Yarn bobbins

gauge
22 sts x 30 rows over stocking stitch = 4"/10 cm using 4 mm (US 6/UK 8) needles

PAJAMA CASE

Using 4 mm (US 6/UK 8) needles, cast on 66 sts.
Now commence pattern as follows:

Row 1 (RS): (K1, p1) to end.

Row 2: As Row 1.

Row 3: (P1, k1) to end.

Row 4: As Row 3.

These four rows set the pattern.

Continue in pattern as set until work measures 24"/60 cm, ending with a WS row.

Keeping pattern correct either side, begin to work flap of case as follows:

Next row: Pattern 8, k50, pattern 8.

Next row: Pattern 8, p50, pattern 8.

Continue as set for a further 16 rows, ending on a WS row.

Now work intarsia rose reading rows on chart from right to left.

Note: A separate ball of the main shade will need to be used either side of the chart and you will also need to wind small balls of the contrast yarns, joining in and breaking off the colors as required.

Row 1 (RS): Pattern 8, k19, work first row of chart over next 17 sts, k14, pattern 8.

Continue working from the chart and at the same time keep the border pattern and stocking stitch either side as set until you have completed the chart.

Using the main shade only, work a further 18 rows. Cast off.

Work lace edging as follows:
Using 3¾ mm (US 5/UK 9) needles, cast on 7 sts.

Row 1 (RS): K1, k2tog, yon twice, k2tog, yon twice, k2.

Row 2: K3, (p1, k2) twice.

Row 3: K1, k2tog, yon twice, k2tog, k4.

Row 4: Cast off 2 sts, k3 (not including st already on needles after casting off), p1, k2.

These 4 rows form the pattern. Rep them until piece is long enough to fit across the cast-off edge of the flap when slightly stretched. Cast off.

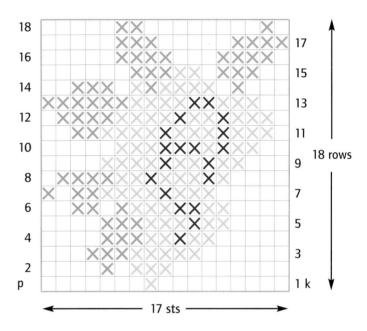

to finish

Work in ends on all pieces. Embroider rose onto center of flap following the chart and using the Swiss darning method (see page 29). Fold pattern piece in half to start of flap. Sew side seams. Take lace and pin in place along cast-off edge. Sew neatly in position. Attach ribbons on each side of flap.

snowdrop cap-sleeve shrug

A mohair mix yarn and large needles are combined to give a light and lacy texture to this pretty shrug. Although a project for the more experienced knitter, it will still be quite quick to make. The snowdrop lace patterning has just eight rows so it is reasonably easy to follow. A neat edging completes the garment.

star rating
★★★ (experienced)

measurements
To fit bust 34–36"/86–92 cm
Actual bust measurement: 36"/91 cm
Length to shoulders: 13"/33 cm
Sleeve seam: 3"/8 cm

materials
- 5 x 1.75 oz/50 g balls of Patons Studio Mohair DK weight (shade 11)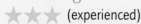
- Pair of 5½ mm (US 9/UK 5) needles
- Pair 5 mm (US 8/UK 6) needles

gauge
17 sts x 24 rows over lacy pattern = 4"/10 cm using 5½ mm (US 9/UK 5) needles

BACK

Using 5½ mm (US 9/UK 5) needles, cast on 77 sts. Purl 1 row.
Now commence pattern as follows:
Row 1 (RS): K1, *yfwd, sl1, k2tog, psso, yfwd, k5. Rep from * to last 4 sts, yfwd, sl1, k2tog, psso, yfwd, k1.
Row 2 and every following alt row: Purl.
Row 3: As Row 1.
Row 5: K4, *yfwd, sl1, k1, psso, k1, k2tog, yfwd, k3. Rep from * to last st, k1.
Row 7: K1, *yfwd, sl1, k2tog, psso, yfwd, k1. Rep from * to end.
Row 8: Purl.
These 8 rows form the pattern and are repeated throughout.
Cont in pattern for a further 3 repeats, ending with Row 8.

Shape armholes

Keeping pattern correct, cast off 8 st at the beg of the next 2 rows. (61 sts.) Cont straight in pattern until work measures 7½"/19 cm ending on a purl row. Cast off fairly loosely.

LEFT FRONT

Using 5½ mm (US 9/UK 5) needles, cast on 20 sts.
Now commence pattern as follows:
Row 1: Knit.
Row 2: K2, purl to last 2 sts, k2.
Rep last 2 rows until work measures 10"/25.5 cm, ending with Row 2.
Next row: Knit, increasing 9 sts evenly across row. (29 st.)
Next row: Purl.
Place a marker at front edge of last row.
Continue in lacy pattern as follows:
Row 1 (RS): K1, *yfwd, sl1, k2tog, psso, yfwd, k5. Rep from * to last 4 sts, yfwd, sl1, k2tog, psso, yfwd, k1.
Row 2 and every following alt row: Purl.
Row 3: As Row 1.
Row 5: K4, *yfwd, sl1, k1, psso, k1, k2tog, yfwd, k3. Rep from * to last st, k1.
Row 7: K1, *yfwd, sl1, k2tog, psso, yfwd, k1. Rep from * to end.
Row 8: Purl.
These 8 rows form the pattern and are repeated throughout.
Cont in pattern as set for a further 5 repeats, ending with Row 8. ***

Shape armholes

Cast off 8 sts at beg of next row.
Cont in pattern until front measures the same as back to shoulder, ending on a purl row. Cast off.

RIGHT FRONT

Work as right front to ***.
Next row: Work Row 1 of pattern.

Shape armholes

Cast off 8 sts at beg of next row. (21 sts.)
Cont in pattern until front measures the same as back to shoulder, ending on a purl row. Cast off.

SLEEVES (Make 2 alike)

Using 5½ mm (US 9/UK 5) needles, cast on 69 sts, knit 4 rows in garter stitch.
Now commence pattern as follows:
Row 1 (RS): K1, *yfwd, sl1, k2tog, psso, yfwd, k5. Rep from * to last 4 sts, yfwd, sl1, k2tog, psso, yfwd, k1.
Row 2 and every following alt row: Purl.
Row 3: As Row 1.
Row 5: K4, *yfwd, sl1, k1, psso, k1, k2tog, yfwd, k3. Rep from * to last st, k1.
Row 7: K1, *yfwd, sl1, k2tog, psso, yfwd, k1. Rep from * to end.
Row 8: Purl.
These 8 rows form the pattern and are repeated throughout.
Cont in pattern for a further 2 repeats, ending with Row 8.
Cast off.

EDGING

Back hem edging

Using 5 mm (US 8/UK 6) needles and with RS facing, rejoin yarn and pick up and knit 77 sts across lower edge of back. Cast off as follows: *cast off 2 sts, sl st back onto left-hand needle, cast on 2 sts, cast off 4 sts. Rep from * to end.

Left front edging

Using 5 mm (US 8/UK 6) needles and with RS facing, rejoin yarn at left shoulder. Pick up and knit approx 3 sts from every 4 rows down front edge to marker. Work cast-off row as on back edging.

Right front and back neck edging

Sew up right shoulder seam. Using 5 mm (US 8/UK 6) needles and with RS facing, rejoin yarn at marker, pick up and knit approx 3 sts from every 4 rows up right front to shoulder, pick up 27 sts from back neck. Work cast-off edge as for back hem.

to finish

Sew up left shoulder seam. Place center of sleeve tops to shoulder seams, then sew sleeves evenly to back and front. Sew last 8 rows of sleeve to cast off sts of backs and fronts. Now join side and sleeve seams for 4 pattern repeats.

sweetheart legwarmers

Toning shades of pink are combined along with Fair Isle patterning to create these gorgeous feminine legwarmers. Knitted in the softest pure wool they will keep you toasty warm on cooler days. Little hearts are knitted and sewn onto the ties to add extra embellishment.

star rating
★★★ (experienced)

measurements
Width: 13"/33 cm
Length: 17"/43 cm

materials
- 2 x 1.75 oz/50 g balls of Rowan Pure Wool 4-ply (shade A, 428 Raspberry)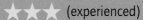
- 1 x 1.75 oz/50 g ball of Rowan Pure Wool 4-ply (shade B, 443 Powder)
- 1 x 1.75 oz/50 g ball of Rowan Pure Wool 4-ply (shade C, 449 Vintage)
- Pair of 3¾ mm (UK 9/US 5) needles
- Small amount of stuffing

gauge
26 sts x 34 rows over stocking stitch = 4"/10 cm using 3¾ mm (US 5/UK 9) needles

Note: Fair Isle is worked using the stranding method: yarn is carried fairly loosely across the back of the work, catching in on every 4th st when needed. Take care not to pull yarn too tightly as this will result in puckering of the fabric. Patterning is worked from appropriate charts, reading the rows from right to left on knit rows and left to right on purl rows.

LEGWARMERS (Make 2 alike)

Using 3¾ mm (US 5/UK 9) needles and shade C, cast on 80 sts fairly loosely.

Commence pattern as follows:

Work 2 rows k2, p2 rib. Change to shade B.

Work 4 rows k2, p2 rib. Change to shade A.

Work 10 rows k2, p2 rib.

Change to st st and continue in shade A.

Beginning with a Knit row, work 16 rows st st.

Join in shade B and work 4 rows from Chart B. Break shade B.

Continue in shade A and work a further 10 rows st st. Join in shade C.

Now work 9 rows from Heart Chart A. Break shade C.

Continue in shade A and work 11 rows st st. Join in shade B.

Now work 4 rows from Chart B. Break shade B.

Continue in shade A and work 10 rows st st. Join in shade C.

Now work 9 rows from Heart Chart A. Break shade C.

Continue in shade A and work 11 rows st st. Join in shade B.

Now work 4 rows from Chart B. Break shade B.

Continue in shade A and work 16 rows st st.

Now work 10 rows k2, p2 rib, break shade A, join in shade B.

Now work 4 rows k2, p2 rib, break shade B, join in shade C.

Work 2 rows k2, p2 rib, cast off in rib.

Hearts (Make 2 in each of shades B and C)

Using 3¾ mm (US 5/UK 9) needles, cast on 2 sts.

Row 1: Inc knitways in each st.

Row 2: Purl.

Row 3: Inc in first st, k to last 2 sts, inc in last st.

Row 4: Purl.

Rep last 2 rows 4 times more. (14 sts.)

Next row: K2tog, k5 and turn, leaving remaining 7 sts on the needle.

Next row: P2tog, p2, p2tog.

Cast off 4 sts.

Return to remaining stitches, rejoin yarn and proceed as follows:

Next row: K5, k2tog.

Next row: P2tog, p2, p2tog.

Cast off 4 sts.

to finish

Work in all ends neatly. Sew seam of legwarmers, matching patterns and colors as you do so. Sew tiny hearts together in pairs, RS facing inside. Leave a small opening to allow you to turn the heart to the right side. Place a small piece of stuffing inside the heart and then sew up the opening. Make 3 other hearts in the same way. Make a twisted cord approximately 30"/76 cm long. Using a blunt-ended needle, thread the cord through the knitting just below the rib, tie at the side of the leg. Attach a heart to each end of the cord. Make another cord the same and thread through the second legwarmer.

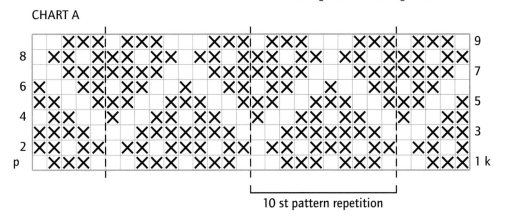

CHART A

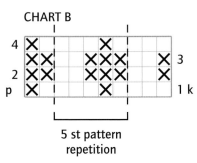

CHART B

5 st pattern repetition

10 st pattern repetition

Acknowledgments

My thanks go to the following people for their help and encouragement during the time I worked on this book:
Coats Patons and Rowan Yarns for their kind donation of some of the yarns for the projects in my book. Pat Benison, Julie Ogden and Kat Arney for their help with a few of the knitted projects. Corinne Masciocchi and the team at New Holland Publishing without whose help and guidance this book would not have been possible; Mark Winwood for his wonderful photography. And last but not least my dear friends and family who have been supportive and patient throughout all the work involved.

Knitting needle size chart

Metric (MM)	US	UK/Canadian
2 mm	0	14
2$\frac{1}{4}$ mm	1	13
2$\frac{3}{4}$ mm	2	12
3 mm	2/3	11
3$\frac{1}{4}$ mm	3	10
3$\frac{3}{4}$ mm	5	9
4 mm	6	8
4$\frac{1}{2}$ mm	7	7
5 mm	8	6
5$\frac{1}{2}$ mm	9	5
6 mm	10	4
6$\frac{1}{2}$ mm	10$\frac{1}{2}$	3
7 mm	10$\frac{1}{2}$	2
7$\frac{1}{2}$ mm	11	1
8 mm	11	0
9 mm	13	00
10 mm	15	000

Yarn Weight Symbol & Category Names	0 lace	1 super fine	2 fine	3 light	4 medium	5 bulky	6 super bulky
Type of Yarns in Category	Fingering 10-count crochet thread	Sock, Fingering, Baby	Sport, Baby	DK, Light Worsted	Worsted, Afghan, Aran	Chunky, Craft, Rug	Bulky, Roving

Source: Craft Yarn Council of America's www.YarnStandards.com

Index